HELP!

My Apartment Has a Dining Room Cookbook

HELP!

My Apartment Has a Dining Room Cookbook

How to Have People Over Without Stressing Out
100+ Foolproof Recipes

KEVIN MILLS AND NANCY MILLS

ILLUSTRATIONS BY RICHARD GOLDBERG

HOUGHTON MIFFLIN COMPANY
Boston   New York
1999

For information about permission to reproduce selections from this book, write to Permissions, Houghton Mifflin Company, 215 Park Avenue South, New York, New York 10003.

Library of Congress Cataloging-in-Publication Data

Mills, Kevin, date.
    Help! My apartment has a dining room cookbook: how to have people over without stressing out: 100+ foolproof recipes / Kevin Mills and Nancy Mills; illustrations by Richard Goldberg.
        p. cm.
    ISBN 0-395-89255-4
    1. Entertaining. 2. Cookery. I. Mills, Nancy, 1942– . II. Title.
TX731.M49 1999
642'.4—dc21   99-12464

HAD 10 9 8 7 6 5 4 3 2 1
Designed by Susan McClellan
Printed in the United States of America

▼

To Martha Mills,
who recently celebrated her 80th birthday and is
an inspiration to us both, inside and out of the kitchen.

▼

To Annabelle Dunhoff,
who would have been very proud of the book.

▼

And, of course, to Jody and Bart,
who were our willing lab rats.

Contents

▲

▼

▼

▼

My Discovery of the Dining Room

A LOT HAS HAPPENED SINCE I WROTE *Help! My Apartment Has a Kitchen* with my mother a few years ago. I turned 25, a milestone to some, especially my insurance company, which feels I'm suddenly a safer driver. I got married to Jody, who's since become a doctor. Our lives haven't changed much; I still do all the cooking, she does the tax returns. But the big change, other than the fact that I now have two Christmas celebrations, is that we got a bigger apartment, one with a great kitchen and an excellent view of runway #2 at the Los Angeles International Airport. I knew that my life had changed forever when I heard myself on the phone bragging to a friend that I have a double oven. The old me wouldn't have had any more use for a double oven than for a tile re-grouter. But the older, wiser me finds it a real convenience and a great time-saver. Some mythical cooking beast has possessed my body. But how bad can that be when I have all this cupboard space?

WHY WOULD I NEED MORE ROOM? After all, I was able to cook for myself, Jody and the occasional transient in our old four-foot cooking box the landlord called a kitchen. But now I can open the fridge and the oven at the same time, an act crucial to all well-oiled cooking operations. The most important benefit of having a kitchen I can yawn in without knocking the spices off the wall is that I can now make more than one dish at a time. And that means I can cook for friends and relatives.

However, inviting people over to eat is more than just a matter of space. For me, it's more basic. I'm still nervous about cooking for anyone who doesn't love me. When I cook for Jody, she's just happy that she doesn't have to enter the kitchen. Even if what I make doesn't turn out well, she laps it up and asks for more. Having my parents over is slightly more pressure, but not much. When I made Hungarian Goulash, my mom was so proud of her little boy that she wanted to take a piece home and attach it to the fridge, next to my old spelling tests. No, the real problems come when I have to cook for outsiders. This is the universal paradox of entertaining: *the less well you know or like the people coming over, the more work you will do to impress them.*

A few weeks after we moved into our apartment, Jody came home from her new job with the big news. She had invited six of her new best friends to dinner that weekend. "Fine," I said—after all, we had discussed this—"Did you tell them it was potluck?"

"Oops," was her response. We knew we had to get to work.

First we had to finish buying furniture. Since Jody and I prefer to eat dinner on the couch in front of the TV, we hadn't gotten around to buying a dinner table. "Who needs one?"

we figured. "Doesn't everyone eat on the couch?" I'm sure even the President wishes he could hold state dinners in the Oval Living Room. But, for some reason, when we have guests for dinner, we hide our primitive instincts and move the action into the most civilized of settings, the Dining Room. Therefore, we had to get ourselves a real table.

Next we planned the menu. Jody and I have a hard enough time compromising on what we're going to make for ourselves, let alone others. I felt the awesome weight of responsibility. The happiness and nourishment of six other human beings was up to us. We finally settled on lasagna, potato salad and bean dip, figuring that if they didn't like it, they could stop at a 7-Eleven on their way home.

It's always worrying to let people into your apartment. A man's home is his pigsty. So, on the day of the big event, we plowed the layers of mess from the living room into the bedroom. While Jody vacuumed and moved the couch to cover the stain on the rug, I took care of the cooking. The thought that calmed me was that whatever happened, I wouldn't have to see these people Monday morning.

When our guests arrived, it was clear that this event meant less to them than it did to us. For them, it was a free meal and a chance to look in our medicine cabinet. They were laughing and joking as if this were just another day, not "D.P. Day" (Dinner Party Day). We started the invasion with the Bean Dip. It was a big success. Pretty soon, we had them eating out of our hands, at least until the dishwasher was done.

SOME PEOPLE, like my mom, have no trouble cooking for company. She'll invite someone to dinner, and at the end of the conversation, she'll add, "Oh, and if you know any marching bands that need to eat, bring them along." But before I'll invite someone over, I have to do a thorough background check, a wiretap and a five-page survey. "What kind of food do you like?" "What color tablecloth do you find most soothing?" "Are you willing to sign a legal waiver?"

My mom has the confidence to decide what to make on the day of the dinner party. She might come across a recipe for Lamb Shazam a few hours before the guests arrive and rush right out to the supermarket. I, on the other hand, test my food with focus groups before I serve it to company.

THIS BOOK IS DESIGNED TO BE HELPFUL to people who get stressed out about having people over. My mom, who is a world-class entertainer as well as a great cook, is a calming voice in the kitchen. Everything I know about entertaining, I learned from her. (Well, everything useful. I learned some things in college, but I can hardly ask my guests to wear togas.) She compiled the recipes, and she offers many tips to make the cooking easier. I road tested all the recipes, getting rid of the fancy cookbook talk. Hopefully, this book will take some of the worry out of the kitchen. But remember, if entertaining were easy, they never would have invented the potluck dinner.

—*Kevin Mills*

Entertaining Basics
Mom Had to Teach Me

Entertaining doesn't mean there has to be a floor show. You don't have to swing from the chandelier in a tuxedo singing show tunes. All you need to do is feed the people, and then they'll leave you alone. The key factor in entertaining is to relax. The worst thing that can happen is that everyone will lose a few pounds.

There's a style of entertaining that involves centerpieces and cloth napkins folded into the shapes of barnyard animals. For me, a few wilting flowers in the middle of the table

are as far as I'll go in decorating. And my guests should be thankful to get a napkin that's clean. If you're concerned about wowing everyone with your élan, you're on your own. Keep in mind that this is your home, and the guests will conform to your style.

That doesn't mean you can just throw food into their mouths from the kitchen. A few simple steps can go a long way toward making sure your guests are happy. This section consists of questions I've had to ask my mom. She's been holding dinner parties since they invented food.

HOW MANY THINGS SHOULD I MAKE?

My first thought is to get by with as little effort as possible. There are one-dish meals you can serve, such as Black Bean Lasagna (page 169) or Mexican Meatball Soup (page 84), that are filling enough to stand alone. But it's a good idea to make at least a couple of dishes, for several reasons:

▼ Some might not turn out. It's the law of averages. The more things you cook, the more likely you are to have a mishap. It's got nothing to do with you. Even Babe Ruth struck out once in a while.

▼ You may hit on the one thing that a guest can't eat because of a traumatic childhood experience.

▼ If there's a vegetarian in the bunch, you need to have some options.

▼ It's a good idea to serve a well-balanced meal in case some of your guests care about nutrition.

▼ It's better to make too much food than too little. If people's stomachs are rumbling during after-dinner conversation, it may drown out your witty banter. Besides, it's your house, so any leftovers belong to you.

HOW DO I CHOOSE THE MENU?

At this stage of the planning, I'm like Hamlet. The first question I ask myself is, "What can I make that I'm sure will turn out OK?" I'm not so confident that I'll try something new for company. Too many things can go wrong. The second question is, "Are the guests friends who'll like me no matter what, or do I have to make an effort?" Your friends will be able to spot your attempts to show off, but you might be able to fool others. Don't agonize too much over what other people want to eat. Make what you like and hope your guests have the same good taste that you do. Here's the mental checklist my mom uses when she has a moment of pause after she drops the invitations in the mail slot and can't take them back:

▼ Don't choose all Not So Easy recipes unless you're a masochist or have lots of help.

▼ Don't choose dishes that all require last-minute preparation. If you're like me, you may be prone to panic if everything you're making is threatening to burn simultaneously. Choose some you can make the day before.

▼ Vary the spiciness of the dishes.

▼ Don't try to make every dish memorable. One, or maybe two, will do. Extravagant desserts like Chocolate Cheesecake (page 292) and Lemon Meringue Pie (page 295) are showstoppers.

▼ Serve a less common, foreign dish. That way, nobody will know what it's supposed to taste like.

▼ Don't make four things that are the same color unless you want to have a color theme.

▼ Keep in mind the temperature outside when you're deciding what to serve. Hearty foods like Chicken with Red Wine (page 228), Lasagna (page 172) and Black Bean Soup (page 76) go down better in cold weather, while lighter foods like Easy Shrimp Creole (page 246), Prosciutto and Melon (page 58) and Greek Salad (page 94) are more suited to hot weather.

▼ Consider a geographical theme; see page 20.

WHAT CAN I MAKE THE NIGHT BEFORE?

Usually, I mock people who prepare ahead of time. I once wrote a semester's worth of journal entries for a creative writing class the night before it was due. But when it comes to dinner parties, you can't ask for an extension. I hate going to someone's house and having to wait hours to eat. So try to get as much done as you can before the guests start ringing the doorbell. Also, it's a good idea to make your mistakes while there's still time to do something about it.

At the top of each recipe, we've noted whether or not the dish can be made partially or entirely in advance. Some dishes, like Beef Bourguignon (page 192) and Chicken with Red Wine (page 228), actually taste better when they've been prepared ahead, while others, like Bruschetta (page 60) and Eggs Benedict (page 262), have to be made right before serving. So pay attention to the notes at the top of each recipe. They're not just for anal-retentives.

HOW DO I MAKE THE FOOD LOOK NICE?

I'm not so concerned with the food being aesthetically pleasing. My friend Scott used to mock me for eating corn right out of the can. For company's sake, though, you need to tame the beast and at least put the food in a dish. I certainly don't bother with garnishes or spend hours designing the plate with a protractor. But there are some simple steps to making food look presentable that don't violate my manhood.

▼ Use a tablecloth. My tabletop has imprints of crossword puzzles on it. There's something about a clean table that inspires confidence.

▼ Get hold of a few eye-catching serving bowls. It's amazing how the human brain works: put spinach in a beat-up old metal dish, and everyone demurs; put it in a ceramic elephant, and people fight for seconds.

▼ A full serving bowl looks better than a half-empty one. If you don't have the right-size bowl, use a smaller one and refill it as needed.

▼ Try to arrange food symmetrically rather than just dumping it onto a platter. Unless you want to be like the guy in *City Slickers* who runs the chuckwagon ("The food is hot, brown and there's plenty of it!"), I suggest you try to make it look nice.

▼ If you use packaged or take-out food, put it in your own bowls. If you serve it in the container with the bar code on it, the spell will be broken.

WHAT ARE MY SERVING OPTIONS?

There are three main options, not including leading the guests through a chute to a trough: serving family-style, serving from the kitchen and serving buffet-style. Each has benefits, but you should make your choice based on the layout of your living space. (I sound like an interior decorator—"Don't put the moose head there! It will clash with the drapes!")

Family-style: Put everything on the table in bowls and platters, and let people help themselves after they're seated. Arguing and nagging are optional.

▼ Serve family-style only if your table is big enough to seat all the guests.

▼ Since you can't control how much food people will take, make sure you have enough. Consider making a few extra portions in case one guest fills her purse with asparagus.

▼ Serving family-style lets guests who are fussy or who have diet restrictions pick what they like. On the other hand, you may need to make more dishes to select from.

▼ The table should be completely set, including dinner plates.

▼ You'll need serving platters and large bowls, plus serving spoons and forks.

▼ Most food can be served family-style. Large pieces of meat should be cut into individual portions before being put on a serving plate. Desserts, especially pies and cakes, can be served individually, with seconds offered family-style.

Serving from the kitchen: You prepare each plate in the kitchen. Extra portions can be put in bowls and set on the table.

▼ You can control the portions better if you dish out the food yourself. This is helpful if you didn't make quite enough and you want to be sure everybody gets some.

▼ Keep the portions small. That way, less food is wasted. Also, if someone doesn't like one of the dishes, it's less obvious.

▼ This is a good solution if you don't have enough serving platters or bowls. (If you do have them, you can avoid having to clean them.)

Buffet-style: Put everything on a counter or table in bowls and platters, and let people walk around and help themselves.

▼ If your table is too small to seat all your guests, serving buffet-style is a practical alternative.

▼ If your table is big enough to seat the guests but too small to hold all the food at the same time, let people serve themselves at a separate table and then sit down at the dining room table.

▼ You can include the stovetop as part of the buffet if you're serving hot soup or a dish like Chicken and Sausage Gumbo (page 234) that needs to be kept warm.

▼ A buffet is good if people want to eat at different times (for instance, if you have friends over for the Super Bowl).

▼ Set out plates, silverware, napkins and salt and pepper in the buffet area. Drinks and dessert can be set out in a different place so everyone isn't clustered around the wine.

▼ A buffet allows you the option of offering untraditional meals made up of appetizers, several different brunch dishes or desserts.

▼ If you want people to take less, give them smaller plates.

▼ Don't let perishable food sit out for hours. Refrigerate it as soon as people have finished eating.

HOW CAN I STRETCH A MEAL IF THERE'S NOT ENOUGH FOOD?

▼ Make one more easy dish (salad, rice, potatoes).

▼ Serve lots of bread.

▼ Offer cheese as an appetizer (it's very filling).

▼ Bring out peanuts or salsa and chips.

▼ Cut any meat into smaller pieces.

▼ Serve the portions yourself to make sure it all goes around.

▼ Use smaller plates.

▼ Tell some of your guests to go home. First come, first served.

HOW DO I KEEP COSTS DOWN?

It's important to keep in mind, as you're lamenting how full your grocery cart is, that it would be a lot more expensive if you were taking all your guests out to a restaurant. However, there are ways to save money.

▼ Decide your menu based on what's cheap at the store. Some days, chicken is on sale; other days, beef is a better value. My mom shops according to the grocery ads and coupons. I tend to use those sections to line the birdcage. You may be the type of person who will drive miles out of your way for a bargain. But if you are, you don't need me to tell you about coupons.

▼ Consider buying meats, fruits and vegetables in bulk packages; they're cheaper per pound.

▼ When you plan the menu, remember that some foods, including strawberries, corn, melon, asparagus and salmon, are cheaper at certain times of the year than others.

▼ Choose dishes that call for inexpensive cuts of meat. Southern Barbecued Pork (page 210) and Old-Fashioned Brisket with Barbecue Sauce (page 200) have to be cooked longer, but unless you're shopping an hour before the guests arrive, that shouldn't be a problem.

▼ Serve a pasta dish. One of the reasons Lasagna (page 172) is so popular is that it's cheap.

▼ If you're serving an expensive seafood like shrimp, start with a hearty soup so people won't be too hungry.

▼ Serve a one-dish meal. Choices include Mexican Meatball Soup (page 84), Greek Salad (page 94), Salade Niçoise (page 106), Lasagna (page 172), Black Bean Lasagna (page 169), Cheese Fondue (page 176), Eggplant Parmesan (page 180), Spicy Lentils and Spinach (page 184), Chicken and Sausage Gumbo (page 234) and Easy Shrimp Creole (page 246).

▼ Do your entertaining at brunch. People eat less during the middle of the day, and brunch foods are generally less expensive. Here are some dishes that work for brunch: Blinis (page 265), Blueberry Waffles (page 258), Eggs Benedict (page 262), Greek Salad (page 94), Honey Spice Bread (page 134), Omelets (page 260), Prosciutto and Melon (page 58), Salade Niçoise (page 106) and Spinach Quiche (page 268).

▼ When guests ask whether they can bring anything, say, "Cash."

A FINAL WORD

It's not as hard as it sounds to cook for a group. Other people's expectations won't be as high as yours. But if all this planning ahead isn't calming you down, skip to the wine section (page 27).

Around the World Without Leaving the Dining Room

Asian

▼

French

▼

Middle Eastern

▼

Indian

▼

Spicy Potatoes *(page 120)*

Lemon Rice *(page 122)*

Gujerati Beans *(page 148)*

Onion and Leek Curry *(page 154)*

Stuffed Peppers *(page 186)*

Tandoori Chicken *(page 231)*

Italian

▼

Prosciutto and Melon *(page 58)*

Bruschetta *(page 60)*

Onion Focaccia *(page 62)*

Minestrone *(page 72)*

Angel Hair Pasta with Tomatoes and Basil
(page 158)

Pasta with Mushrooms and Artichokes *(page 160)*

Penne Arrabbiata *(page 162)*

Tortellini with Creamy Tomato Sauce *(page 164)*

Lasagna *(page 172)*

Eggplant Parmesan *(page 180)*

Veal Scallopini with Mustard Sauce *(page 204)*

Mexican

▼

Black Bean Soup *(page 76)*

Tortilla Soup *(page 82)*

Mexican Meatball Soup *(page 84)*

Southwestern Coleslaw *(page 100)*

Corn Bread *(page 132)*

Mexican Grilled Cornish Hens *(page 224)*

Russian

▼

Russian Vegetable Borscht *(page 74)*

Chicken Kiev *(page 237)*

Blinis *(page 265)*

Barbecuing in Front of People

BARBECUING REDUCES COOKING TO ITS BASICS: fire, meat and swear words. If you know what you're doing, barbecuing is as simple as using the oven. If you're new to the sport, it's easy to char your food beyond the point where a dog will eat it. But it's worth trying to understand the barbecue, because it makes food taste better.

BUYING A GRILL

I've heard of people frying eggs on a hot car engine, but basically, there are two types of grills: charcoal and gas. Gas grills cost a lot more than charcoal ones, but they heat up faster and there's less fiddling. With gas grills, you'll have to replenish your propane supply periodically, but propane is not hard to come by.

Having said that, I have a charcoal grill. To me, it's no fun barbecuing with an on/off switch. You might as well be in the kitchen. With charcoal grills, it's more difficult to light the fire and the grill takes longer to heat up, but it appeals to the primitive instincts that inspire you to barbecue in the first place. Gas grills may be an advancement, but I'll never get rid of my charcoal grill. I'm sure there were Neanderthals who objected to the use of fire at all ("Raw good enough for Og, raw good enough for me!"). I get to choose where progress stops for me.

WHEN DO I START THE FIRE?

With a gas grill, you should fire it up on high about 10 minutes before you start cooking. With a charcoal grill, you'll need about 40 minutes. If you use a charcoal grill, you might also need to factor in some time at the beginning in case you have difficulty lighting the coals.

HOW DO I START THE FIRE?

Gas: Just press the starter button.

Charcoal: First, open the vents at the bottom of the grill. Remove the wire cooking rack and prepare the charcoal briquettes. Depending on the size of your grill, you will need between one-fourth and one-third of a 10-pound bag. You have four options:

▼ Buy a metal fire chimney, available from most hardware stores, large drugstores and specialty food shops for under $15.00. This is a good way to light the fire without using any accelerants or electrical devices. The chimney is a large cylinder that you fill with charcoal and light by igniting newspaper that you've stuffed underneath. Once the briquettes are burning (about 25 minutes), carefully pour them out into the bottom of the grill, one layer deep.

Advantage: Almost always works.

Disadvantages: Initial expense; bulky to store.

▼ Use an electric firestarter, available from some hardware stores for under $20.00. This device should eliminate all doubt about getting that fire started. Plug it in and lay it across the pyramid of briquettes. Be sure to check the instructions—you should always read the instructions on a device called "firestarter."

Advantage: Always works.

Disadvantages: Initial expense; needs nearby electrical outlet.

▼ Use "Ready to Light" charcoal briquettes. These briquettes are supercharged, so there's no need for charcoal starter. Just pile them in a pyramid and light with a match. Fumes from these briquettes can affect the flavor of your dinner, so wait until the briquettes are covered with gray ash before putting food on the grill.

Advantages: Fairly cheap and easily available; always works.

Disadvantages: These burn more quickly than regular briquettes, so heat may die out before you've finished cooking; the food may taste of chemicals.

▼ Pile the briquettes into a pyramid in the middle of the grill. Get your charcoal starter. Squirt the starter onto the briquettes according to the directions. Light a few briquettes with a match. The rest should catch fire quickly. You may have a foot-high blaze for a minute or two, so don't do this under a tree or right next to the house. *Do not add any charcoal starter once the briquettes have caught fire. You want to eat nice home-cooked food, not Jell-O in the burn unit of the hospital.* Fumes from the charcoal starter can make your food taste like, well, charcoal starter, so don't put food on the grill early to give it a head start. The fumes will burn off after a few minutes, as the coals begin to catch fire.

Advantages: Cheap and easily available.

Disadvantage: Sometimes doesn't light immediately.

WHEN DO I PUT THE FOOD ON?

Gas: When you can put your hand over the grill surface and hold it there for only 2 seconds.

Charcoal: Assuming the briquettes catch fire when you first light them, it takes 30 to 40 minutes to get them hot enough to cook with. Once they are covered with gray ash, use metal tongs or a large fork to spread them into a single layer. Put the wire cooking rack on the grill. The temperature should be hot enough so you can't hold your hand over the coals for more than 2 to 3 seconds. If you feel your flesh melting away, it's hot enough.

WHEN DO I TAKE THE FOOD OFF?

The easiest way to check whether meat is cooked is to take it off the grill and cut into it. If it's too rare, throw it back on the fire.

Here are some general tips:

▼ Don't let the food sit on the grill while you go play Ping-Pong. Sometimes the difference between perfection and incineration is a few seconds.

▼ Food in the center of the cooking rack will cook faster than food on the edges.

▼ If the food is cooking too fast and you want to lower the heat, move the coals farther apart and partially close the air vents. Some grills allow you to raise or lower the cooking rack. Moving the food farther from the flame will slow the cooking process.

▼ If the food isn't done when you check it, put it back on the grill—or finish cooking it in the oven at 400 degrees; it will already have the smoky barbecue flavor.

HOW DO I PUT OUT FOOD FIRES?

You have several options. If your grill has a lid, close it or put it on. The flames will immediately cease, although you won't be able to see that happening. If there's no lid, either temporarily remove the food from the grill to a plate or move it to an area where there are fewer coals. Flames usually start when fat drips onto coals, so reduce the chances of this by trimming off the fat beforehand. However, this doesn't work with hamburgers. A spray bottle of water can help spritz out flares. However, *do not* pour water onto the fire, because wet ashes might splash onto the food. And, in any case, it will make a terrible mess.

What do I do with the coals when I'm finished cooking?

If your grill has a lid, close it or put it on. Then shut all the vents, cutting off the oxygen supply. The coals will stop burning, and the remains will be available for your next barbecue. Coals are good until they disappear.

What do I do with the ashes?

After about six barbecues, shovel the ashes out and discard them. Or bury them at sea. But wait until they've cooled off, or until you want to use the grill again.

How do I clean the grill?

With a gas grill, turn the heat to high for 10 minutes, with the lid closed. After the cooking rack cools down or the next day, scrape it clean with crumpled foil or a wire grill brush. If your charcoal grill has a lid, close the lid at the end of grilling. The heat will burn off most of the food. The next day, scrape the cooking rack clean with crumpled foil or a wire grill brush. For grills without a lid, do a lot of scraping the next day.

How dangerous is barbecuing?

Not very, unless you're clumsy and Clouseau-esque. The grill itself is hot, so don't lean up against it or allow defenseless babies near it. It's also dirty, so don't wear your Sunday best. Finally, and this should go without saying, *do not barbecue in the house.* The fumes from burning coals are toxic.

Which recipes in this book are suitable for barbecuing?

Grilled Vegetable Kebabs (page 152), Grilled Leg of Lamb (page 206), Lamb Souvlakia (page 208), Sweet-and-Sour Country-Style Pork Ribs (page 212), Mexican Grilled Cornish Hens (page 224), Barbecued Chicken (page 218), Chicken Satay with Peanut Sauce (page 220) and Grilled Salmon (page 250).

Wine Without Foolishness

WINE CONNOISSEURS read and write books about wine, many of which seem as though they've been written under the influence. Connoisseurs know every vineyard, the good years, the bad years, the type of grape used. They're willing to pay hundreds of dollars for certain vintages. But if your experience with alcohol extends no further than manning the keg at a tailgate party, your knowledge is probably limited.

That's OK. If you're like me, you don't necessarily want to know what was a good year and what was a bad year. You just don't want to look like a fool. In that case, here are some things to avoid:

▼ Don't break off the corkscrew in the cork.
▼ Don't provide a straw with each wine glass.
▼ Don't buy wine in a can.
▼ Don't serve wine with a screw-on top.
▼ Don't shake it.
▼ Don't act like Steve Martin in *The Jerk*: "We don't want this old wine! Bring us some new wine!"

There's no shortcut to becoming a connoisseur, they tell me. But you can avoid embarrassing yourself if you learn a few simple things.

WHAT ARE THE DIFFERENT TYPES OF WINE?

Red, white and rosé. There are also fortified wines like sherry, port and Madeira, which have a higher alcoholic content and are not served with meals.

WHAT WINE GOES WITH WHAT FOOD?

The general rule is that red wine goes with meat, while white wine goes with chicken or fish. Rosé goes well with chicken or salad. With pasta, take your cue from the sauce. If it's a meat sauce, use red. Otherwise, choose white or rosé. It's up to you how closely you want to follow these rules. Just bear in mind that James Bond spotted the villain in *From Russia with Love* when he gave himself away by ordering red wine with fish.

WHAT ARE SOME GOOD WINES TO BUY?

Don't feel as though a bottle of wine has to have dust on it to be acceptable. You can buy a good bottle at the supermarket or liquor store for from $4.00 to $10.00. My guess is that in a taste test, many people wouldn't be able to tell the difference between plain-wrap red wine and a bottle from the Czar's personal wine cellar. But there are some common types of wine that I've done very well with:

Red: At our wedding, the caterer served Merlot, which was a big hit with our friends. There were lots of designated drivers that day. Also, my friend Scott informs me that Cabernet Sauvignon has a following among the cigar-smoking set. My mom often buys the Callaway and Fetzer brands. Both are available at reasonable prices and, in the right quantities, can turn me into an engaging and articulate after-dinner speaker, at least in my own mind.

White: There are several ways to go with whites. I like Chardonnay, which is common and well thought of by people in the know. There are partisans for Chenin Blanc, Pinot Blanc and Sauvignon Blanc. As for specific brands, Scott says, "You will always be on target with Kendall-Jackson Chardonnay at $9.00 to $16.00 per bottle." He didn't talk like that in college.

How much wine should I buy?

A good rule of thumb is half a bottle per drinker. That's two to three glasses. If you know your guests like the sauce, buy more. If Marlon Brando's coming over, the sky's the limit. If you buy too much, start your own wine cellar with the leftovers.

How do I serve wine?

You don't need to walk around the table like a wine steward, showing everyone the label. Just pop the cork and let the guests fight for it. Here are a few other tips:

▼ Take off the price tag. Or replace it with the price tag from your stereo system.
▼ Don't fill wine glasses to the top. Fill them half-full or two-thirds at the most.
▼ Refrigerate white and rosé wines; never refrigerate red wine.

WHAT DO I DO IF I MANGLE THE CORK?

There's no need to throw the bottle away. Pour the wine through a strainer into a serving vessel of some kind. And don't tell anyone. It should taste fine. If someone at the table complains, say that the wine was improperly stored at the liquor store and that you made sure the person responsible was fired.

WHAT DO THESE WINE TERMS MEAN?

Like doctors, wine snobs have their own language. We all know the definition of "hangover," but here are some others:

▼ **"Letting wine breathe"**—an expression relating to taking the cork out a few hours early. Expensive old red wine is supposed to taste better if it breathes.

▼ **"Bouquet"**—a fancy word for how the wine smells. If your nose is untrained, don't worry about it, as long as the wine doesn't smell like vinegar.

▼ **"Body"**—a term relating to the consistency of the wine. Is it thin or full-bodied? Watery or chewy? Connoisseurs love these vocabulary exercises. When I'm the host, if the wine pours when I tip the bottle, it's the right consistency.

Learning to Speak Coffee
(and Tea)

"Excuse me. I'll have a decaf mocha espresso latte cappuccino."

"I'm sorry. I don't speak coffee."

Because I don't drink coffee or tea, I realize my opinions on politics and contemporary life are less valid. I just don't like the taste. But since some people don't consider the meal complete until they've drunk their dirty water, it's a good idea to know your way around coffee beans and tea bags. Just keep in mind that coffee drinkers are like all junkies. If they can't get the best stuff, they'll settle for whatever you have. Offer it when conversation lags after dessert.

The lowest form of coffee is instant. It's also the easiest. Making instant coffee involves spooning a tablespoon of crystals into a mug and adding boiling water. Most sophisticated coffee drinkers scoff at this method. In one comedy sketch, a man in a suit is standing over a man in a hospital bed. The man in the suit says, "We've replaced this man's blood with Folgers crystals. Let's see if he can tell the difference." The formerly comatose man in the bed rises with a big smile on his face. But your guests might not be so happy.

A more advanced way to make coffee is using a plastic filter lined with a filter paper. You put the filter over the cup, put two spoonfuls of ground coffee in the filter paper, pour the boiling water in and let the coffee drip. This way, only the best and most sophisticated flavors make it into the cup. The flavor is good, but the method is slow-going if you have a big crowd.

The next step up the scale is to use machinery. Electric coffeemakers are fairly inexpensive and allow you to make enough coffee for several addicts at once. Just follow the directions that come with the equipment. The flavor is pretty good—this is your average restaurant coffee—and you can make a lot at once.

You can also get an espresso machine, which can cost anywhere from $75.00 to $500.00. My dad has one, and he swears that the coffee it produces drips straight from heaven. When he starts talking like that, we usually tell him to switch to decaf. I borrow his machine on occasion, when I have coffee snobs coming over. He had to teach me how to use it—which was the first time since he'd taught me how to ride a bike that my dad knew more about a contraption than me. But he proudly showed me the technique, and soon my guests were scalding their lips on the best coffee in town. Each machine is different, though, so follow the instructions that come with yours.

You can buy already ground coffee or buy the beans and grind them yourself in a coffee grinder. Grinding beans will impress the guests. It also makes a great sound. Have sugar and milk or cream handy.

I'm not a big fan of tea either. Perhaps it's because as a kid I got sick on the spinning teacup ride at Disneyland. I don't know. But tea is actually quite simple to make.

Tea bags come in many different flavors, with names like English Breakfast or Orange Pekoe.

All you have to do is put the tea bag into a mug and add boiling water. The longer you leave the tea bag in the cup, the stronger the tea will be. Three to five minutes is the optimum; after that, the tea will become bitter. You can also put two or three tea bags inside a teapot, fill it with boiling water and let it sit for a couple of minutes to brew. Serve when the guests just can't wait anymore, and offer milk, sugar, lemon and/or honey.

If you really want to impress, let your guests watch you prepare loose tea in a china teapot. First you need the teapot—easily acquired at a department store or from your grandmother. Packets or boxes of loose tea are available at the grocery store or at specialty coffee-tea shops. In order to keep the tea leaves from getting into individual cups, you should consider buying a tea ball, a small, round metal gadget that opens in the middle and has either lots of small holes in it or mesh sides. Or buy a small tea strainer, through which you can pour the brewed tea.

To make the tea, pour a cup of boiling water into the teapot, swish it around and then pour it into the sink. This heats the pot. Then open the tea ball and fill it with tea leaves (1 teaspoon per person plus 1 for the pot). Snap the tea ball shut and put it inside the teapot. Or if you don't have a tea ball, put the leaves directly into the pot. Pour in 1 cup boiling water per person. Put the lid on and brew for 3 to 5 minutes; any longer will make the tea bitter. If you have a tea cozy—one of those funny-shaped quilted covers—put it on top of the teapot to keep it warm and take it to the table. Remove the cozy before pouring the tea. If the leaves are loose, pour the tea through a strainer into the cups.

Menus for Entertaining

WHEN YOU'RE FEEDING COMPANY, decide on your main dish first. Then figure out what other dishes go with it. You can start the meal with an appetizer, a soup or a salad. To save yourself aggravation: choose at least one recipe you can make the day before; choose recipes that use in-season fruit or vegetables; don't choose all Not So Easy recipes; and don't choose more than one dish that has to be made at the last minute.

▼

Prosciutto and Melon *(page 58)*
Lasagna *(page 172)*
Caesar Salad *(page 92)*
Chocolate Shortbread *(page 278)*

▼

Artichoke Dip *(page 46)*
Beef Bourguignon *(page 192)*
Garlic Mashed Potatoes *(page 116)*
Green Salad with Easy Italian Dressing *(page 109)*
Chocolate Cheesecake *(page 292)*

▼

Creamy Mushroom Soup *(page 68)*
Chicken Kiev *(page 237)*
Plain Rice
Gingery Carrots *(page 146)*
Chocolate Fondue *(page 282)*

▼

Baba Ghanouj *(page 48)*
Barbecued Chicken *(page 218)*
Tabouli Salad *(page 102)*
Corn Bread *(page 132)*
Apple Crisp *(page 272)*

▼

Salmon Spread *(page 56)*
Easy Shrimp Creole *(page 246)*
Caribbean Rice *(page 124)*
Speedy Zucchini *(page 144)*
Lemon Meringue Pie *(page 295)*

▼

Spinach Dip *(page 52)*
Tandoori Chicken *(page 231)*
Pacific Rim Rice Pilaf *(page 126)*
Gujerati Beans *(page 148)*
Chocolate-Raspberry Linzertorte *(page 289)*

Boston Clam Chowder *(page 78)*
Grilled Salmon *(page 250)*
Spicy Potatoes *(page 120)*
Spinach and Strawberry Salad *(page 96)*
Gingerbread *(page 276)*

Mexican Meatball Soup *(page 84)*
Corn Bread *(page 132)*
Caesar Salad *(page 92)*
Chocolate Cake with Buttercream Icing *(page 284)*

Lamb Souvlakia *(page 208)*
Grilled Vegetable Kebabs *(page 152)*
Jody's Potato Salad *(page 104)*
Foolproof Fudge *(page 280)*

Vegetarian Menus

Tortilla Soup *(page 82)*
Mushroom Turnover *(page 178)*
Honey Spice Bread *(page 134)*
Pears in Red Wine *(page 274)*

Hummus *(page 50)*
Eggplant Parmesan *(page 180)*
Tabouli Salad *(page 102)*
Gingerbread *(page 276)*

Bruschetta *(page 60)*
Black Bean Lasagna *(page 169)*

Southwestern Coleslaw *(page 100)*
Apple Crisp *(page 272)*

Onion Focaccia *(page 62)*
Angel Hair Pasta with Tomatoes and Basil
(page 158)
Caesar Salad (omit the anchovies, *page 92*)
Foolproof Fudge *(page 280)*

Black Bean Soup *(page 76)*
Greek Salad *(page 94)*
Chocolate Shortbread *(page 278)*

Minestrone *(page 72)*
Spinach Quiche *(page 268)*
Pears in Red Wine *(page 274)*

Brunch Menus

Eggs Benedict *(page 262)*
Spinach and Strawberry Salad *(page 96)*
Apple Crisp *(page 272)*

Russian Vegetable Borscht *(page 74)*
Blinis *(page 265)*
Seasonal Fresh Fruit

Caesar Salad *(page 92)*
Omelets *(page 260)*
Honey Spice Bread *(page 134)*

Rating the Recipes

WE'VE DIVIDED THE RECIPES INTO THREE CLASSIFICATIONS: **Very Easy, Easy** and **Not So Easy**. I tend toward the Very Easy recipes. It's just like when I read a collection of short stories—I'll always read the shortest one first. I figure if it made it into the book, it must be the same quality as the others. That definitely holds true for the shortest recipes in this book. They can usually be done in about 10 minutes.

Easy recipes require 10 to 15 minutes more of your time, but not much more effort.

"Not So Easy" is not a euphemism for difficult. It just means that you have to watch the food, not the TV. But the recipes are good enough that I'll make the extra effort. The Not So Easy recipes also tend to look impressive and feed a lot of people.

▼▼▼

NOT SO EASY

▲▲▲

Dishes You Can Prepare the Day Before

W HEN YOU'RE FEEDING A GROUP, your life will be a lot easier if you make one or two dishes the day before. Of course, not every dish holds up well overnight. Lemon Meringue Pie (page 295), for instance, is unlikely to impress anyone on Day 2. Lamb Souvlakia (page 208) tastes best right off the grill. However, more than half of the recipes in this book can be made the day before and will taste as good, if not better, because of the wait. There's just one problem about making them early—you might be tempted to eat them that night.

Vegetarian Dishes

APPETIZERS

Artichoke Dip *(page 46)*

Baba Ghanouj *(page 48)*

Bruschetta *(page 60)*

Hummus *(page 50)*

Onion Focaccia *(page 62)*

Spinach Dip *(page 52)*

SOUPS

Black Bean Soup *(page 76)*

Creamy Mushroom Soup
(page 68)

Leek and Potato Soup *(page 70)*

Minestrone *(page 72)*

Russian Vegetable Borscht
(page 74)

Tortilla Soup *(page 82)*

Untraditional Matzo Ball Soup
(page 86)

SALADS / SALAD DRESSINGS

Broccoli, Avocado and Tomato
Salad *(page 98)*

Caesar Salad (omit the anchovies;
page 92)

Greek Salad *(page 94)*

Jody's Potato Salad *(page 104)*

Salade Niçoise (omit the tuna;
page 106)

Southwestern Coleslaw
(page 100)

Spinach and Strawberry Salad
(page 96)

Tabouli Salad *(page 102)*

Easy Italian Dressing *(page 109)*

Simple French Dressing
(page 110)

Thousand Island Dressing
(page 111)

SAUCES

Barbecue Sauce *(page 203)*

Ginger Soy Sauce *(page 242)*

Peanut Sauce *(page 222)*

Sweet-and-Sour Sauce
(page 214)

POTATOES / RICE / BREAD

Caribbean Rice *(page 124)*

Corn Bread *(page 132)*

Fried Potatoes and Onions
(page 114)

Garlic Mashed Potatoes
(page 116)

Honey Spice Bread *(page 134)*

Lebanese Spiced Rice *(page 128)*

Lemon Rice *(page 122)*

Middle Eastern Bulgur Wheat
Pilaf *(page 130)*

Pacific Rim Rice Pilaf *(page 126)*

Potatoes au Gratin *(page 118)*

Spicy Potatoes *(page 120)*

VEGETABLES

PASTA AND VEGETARIAN MAIN DISHES

BRUNCH

Appetizers

WHEN I WAS GROWING UP, "Don't fill up on bread" was up there with "Look both ways" and "Stop hitting your sister" in parental warnings. The theory was that you wanted to leave room for the rest of the meal. Now that I'm older, that piece of guidance makes as little sense as it did then. Heaven forbid, you would get full while eating a meal. I say, if you like the appetizer, eat as much as you can. The main dish might not be edible.

When cooking for company, bringing out the appetizer is like the first day of school. Everyone is judging you, and in the first 30 seconds, you'll find out if you're going to be an emotionally healthy person for the rest of your life or if you're going to be sitting alone on the bus, daydreaming about how they'll all be sorry. These appetizers can't do anything about mismatched clothing or a poorly timed nosebleed, but your guests should be looking forward to the next course.

▲

Recipes

▼

Artichoke Dip

SERVES: 8

Serve with: Veal Scallopini with Mustard Sauce (page 204)
Preparation Time: 10 minutes (using a blender or food processor) or 15 minutes (by hand)
Cooking Time: 30 minutes ▼ Rating: Very Easy
Can Prepare the Day Before: Yes (but bake just before serving)

I'VE ALWAYS BEEN AGAINST ARTICHOKES. I never liked the idea of pulling off a leaf and scraping my teeth on it. It just didn't seem like a modern human activity. Then one evening, our friends the Grahams brought this dip over for dinner. Before I knew what it was, it was too late. I already liked it.

1   teaspoon corn oil or vegetable oil
1   13¾-ounce can artichoke hearts (see Mom Tip 1)
½   cup mayonnaise
6   tablespoons grated Parmesan cheese
    Carrot/celery sticks or box of round melba toasts
    (see Mom Tip 2)

Preheat the oven to 350 degrees. Add the oil to a 1-quart casserole dish and spread it around with a piece of paper towel, making sure to oil the sides as well as the bottom. Set aside.

Drain and discard the liquid from the artichoke hearts.

With a blender or food processor: Combine the artichoke hearts, mayonnaise and Parmesan cheese in the appliance bowl. Blend at high speed for about 20 seconds, or until the mixture is smooth.

By hand: Chop the artichokes as fine as possible and then combine with the mayonnaise and Parmesan cheese in a small bowl.

Transfer the mixture to the casserole dish, spread evenly and bake, uncovered, for about 30 minutes, or until the top begins to brown. Let cool for 5 minutes and serve with carrot/celery sticks or melba toasts. For another way to make this appetizer, see Mom Tip 3.

MOM TIP 1
▼

Artichoke hearts are available in two forms: plain or marinated. For this recipe, get the plain. They are available in cans (with the other canned vegetables) or frozen in boxes (with the other frozen vegetables). Canned artichoke hearts can be used straight from the can, but frozen ones must be cooked (follow the directions on the box) before using. Marinated artichokes, which are soaked in oil and spices, are good in salads, but their oily flavor doesn't work in this dish.

MOM TIP 2
▼

Melba toasts are miniature slices of toast. They come in rounds and rectangles, have little flavor and are very crisp (unless you leave the package open for a few days). They are available in boxes on the cracker shelf.

MOM TIP 3
▼

For individual appetizers: Place a rack 3 inches from the broiling unit and preheat the broiler. Drain the liquid from the artichoke hearts. Cut the hearts into quarters and set aside. Combine the mayonnaise and Parmesan cheese in a medium bowl and mix thoroughly. Add the artichoke hearts and stir gently, making sure each heart is covered with the mayonnaise mixture. Place 28 to 32 melba toasts on an ungreased cookie sheet and spoon 1 artichoke quarter onto each toast. Spoon on any extra mayonnaise mixture. Place the cookie sheet on the oven rack and broil until the tops start to brown, about 1 minute. Check frequently to make sure the toasts don't burn. Serve immediately, with napkins.

Baba Ghanouj

SERVES: 4-6

Serve with: Sweet-and-Sour Country-Style Pork Ribs (page 212)

Preparation Time: 10 minutes (using a blender or food processor) or 15 minutes (by hand)

Cooking Time: 20 minutes ▼ Rating: Easy ▼ Can Prepare the Day Before: Yes

I LIKED BABA GHANOUJ FOR YEARS without knowing what it was made of. But that's the thing about learning to cook. It's a loss of innocence. When the wool was pulled away from my eyes, I discovered that this Middle Eastern dip is made of eggplant.

    1   eggplant (about 1 pound)
    1   garlic clove
    ½   teaspoon salt
    2   tablespoons sesame paste (see Mom Tip 1, page 51)
    2   tablespoons lemon juice
        Dash black pepper
    1   tablespoon chopped fresh parsley (optional)
        Pita bread (see Mom Tip 2, page 51)

Place a rack 3 inches from the broiling unit and preheat the broiler.

Cut off and discard the stem from the eggplant and cut the eggplant lengthwise in half. Put a piece of foil on a cookie sheet and place the eggplant halves, cut side down, on the foil. Broil for 20 minutes, or until the skin has wrinkled and the flesh is very soft. Remove from the oven and let cool.

Peel off and discard the eggplant skin. Squeeze the pulp to get rid of as much juice as possible. Set aside.

Peel and finely chop the garlic and mix it with the salt (see Mom Tip).

With a blender or food processor: Put the eggplant, garlic mixture, sesame paste, lemon juice and pepper in the appliance bowl and process for about 1 minute, or until smooth. Transfer the mixture to a small serving bowl.

By hand: Mash the eggplant in a small bowl as fine as you can with a fork. Add the garlic mixture, sesame paste, lemon juice and pepper and mix thoroughly.

Decorate with the chopped parsley. Serve at room temperature with pita bread.

MOM TIP

▼

I recently read that adding salt directly to the garlic
spreads the flavor of the garlic. It seems to work—
this Baba Ghanouj tastes nicely garlicky.

Hummus

SERVES: 6-8

Serve with: Chicken Sultana (page 226)

Preparation Time: 10 minutes (using a blender or food processor) or 20 minutes (by hand)

Cooking Time: None ▼ Rating: Very Easy ▼ Can Prepare the Day Before: Yes

THE FIRST TIME I HAD HUMMUS was with my in-laws. They had spent two years in Israel many years earlier and had been searching for the Lost Hummus ever since. Then they found a little deli several miles away that they make regular pilgrimages to. I liked it right away and learned to make the dip myself. I hope my in-laws approve.

I pronounce the H in hummus the same as the H in happy. But I think the correct pronunciation requires you to have a sore throat. Sort of like "Hcczummus." Say it as if you're trying to scare away some pigeons.

1	15½-ounce can garbanzo beans (also called chickpeas)
2	garlic cloves
½	cup lemon juice from 2-3 lemons
½	cup sesame paste (see Mom Tip 1)
¼	teaspoon salt (or more to taste)
1-2	tablespoons water (optional)
1	teaspoon olive oil
¼	teaspoon paprika
1	tablespoon chopped fresh parsley (optional)
	Pita bread (see Mom Tip 2)

Drain the garbanzo beans and discard the liquid. Peel the garlic.

With a blender or food processor: Put the garbanzo beans and garlic in the appliance bowl. Add the lemon juice, sesame paste and salt and process for about 1 minute, or until smooth. If the mixture is too thick to process, add a little of the water and process until smooth.

By hand: Mash the garbanzo beans into a paste in a small bowl using a fork. Finely chop the garlic and add it to the mashed beans. Add the lemon juice, sesame paste and salt and mix thoroughly.

Taste to see if the hummus needs more salt and add more if necessary. Transfer the mixture to a wide flat dish and spread it out to a thickness of about 1 inch.

Mix the olive oil with the paprika, pour it over the top of the bean mixture and stir slightly to incorporate. Decorate with the chopped parsley. Serve with wedges of pita bread.

Mom Tip 1

▼

Sesame paste, also known as tahini, is made of ground sesame seeds. It has a nutty flavor and the consistency of peanut butter. Because it has a tendency to separate, mix it thoroughly with a spoon before using. Sesame paste can usually be found in the gourmet or Asian food section of the grocery store or in delicatessens. It comes in cans and jars.

Mom Tip 2

▼

Pita bread, also known as pocket bread, is flat and round and is available in the bread section. It is sold in packages of 4 or more breads, in white and whole wheat varieties.

Spinach Dip

SERVES: 4

Serve with: Chicken and Sausage Gumbo (page 234) ▼ Preparation Time: 15 minutes

Cooking Time: 6 minutes ▼ Waiting Time: 1 hour (optional) ▼ Rating: Very Easy

Can Prepare the Day Before: Yes

IF OLIVE OYL EVER STOPPED FLIRTING WITH BLUTO and committed to Popeye, she would soon find that his addiction to this vegetable stimulant prevented her from reaching him emotionally. OK, so spinach isn't the answer to all your problems, but it does make a good dip.

1   10-ounce package frozen chopped spinach

1   scallion

1   garlic clove

½   cup fresh parsley leaves (see Mom Tip 2, page 103)

⅓   cup mayonnaise

2   tablespoons sour cream or plain yogurt

1   teaspoon salt

½   teaspoon dried dill

¼   teaspoon black pepper

    Crackers

Cook the spinach according to the package directions (about 6 minutes); drain (see Mom Warning). Set aside in a bowl.

Wash the scallion. Cut off and discard the root tip and the top 2 inches of the green part. Cut the remaining white and green parts into ¼-inch pieces and add them to the spinach. Peel and finely chop the garlic and add it to the spinach.

Wash the parsley and pat it dry between paper towels. Cut off and discard the stems and cut the leafy parts into ¼-inch pieces. Add to the spinach.

Add the mayonnaise, sour cream or yogurt, salt, dill and pepper and mix thoroughly. If possible, cover and refrigerate for at least 1 hour to let the flavors develop. However, if you are in a hurry, you can serve it immediately. Serve with crackers.

Mom Warning

▼

Make sure to press out as much water as possible
from the spinach so the dip won't be too runny.
Put the cooked spinach in a strainer and press firmly
against the leaves with the back of a large spoon.

Old-Country Pâté

SERVES: 6-8

Serve with: Old-Fashioned Brisket with Barbecue Sauce (page 200)

Preparation Time: 10 minutes (using a blender or food processor) or 15 minutes (by hand)

Cooking Time: 25 minutes ▼ Rating: Very Easy ▼ Can Prepare the Day Before: Yes

WHEN MY MOM WAS GROWING UP, my grandmother served a regular rotation of meat loaf, Chef Boyardee canned spaghetti and something Mom remembers as "greasy bone-marrow soup." Grandma would also make this great pâté. A few years ago, she proudly showed me how to prepare it. As she fried and ground up the chicken livers, she told me about how her own grandmother had brought the recipe with her to this country. Because I liked it so much, I will always think of Grandma as an accomplished chef, despite my mom's "facts."

There was an episode of *Happy Days* where Fonzie declares that liver isn't cool. Sorry, Fonz, but if my grandma says liver's cool, it's cool.

1	large onion
¼	cup (½ stick) butter or margarine
1	pound chicken livers (see Mom Tip)
½	teaspoon salt
¼	teaspoon black pepper
	Toast or crackers

Peel the onion and cut it into ½-inch pieces. Melt the butter or margarine in a large frying pan over medium heat. Add the onion and cook for about 5 minutes, stirring occasionally, until softened.

Add the chicken livers and cook for about 20 minutes, turning frequently so they don't burn. The livers and onions will get very brown. Remove from the heat.

With a blender or food processor: Transfer the entire contents of the pan—livers, onions and juices—to the appliance bowl. Blend or process for about 10 seconds, or until smooth.

By hand: Mash the mixture thoroughly with a fork in a small bowl.

Season with the salt and pepper and transfer to a serving bowl. Serve warm or chilled with toast or crackers.

MOM TIP

▼

Chicken livers are sold in 1-pound plastic tubs
in the meat department. If none are out on display,
ask the butcher to get you some. Or if you buy whole
chickens frequently, save the livers in a plastic bag in
the freezer until you collect enough to make pâté.

Salmon Spread

SERVES: 6-8

Serve with: Grilled Leg of Lamb (page 206) ▼ Preparation Time: 20 minutes ▼ Cooking Time: None

Waiting Time: 2 hours ▼ Rating: Easy ▼ Can Prepare the Day Before: Yes

SALMON SPREAD IS A CHRISTMAS TRADITION at my grandmother's house, and I think we'd all give up the presents before we'd give it up. The best indicator of how good it is is that it tastes good even when eating is the furthest thing from my mind. I'm now 26, but I admit that on Christmas morning, I still stuff myself full of chocolate. By the early afternoon, my stomach has ballooned. But I still have enough stamina to elbow my loved ones out of the way to get at the Salmon Spread.

"Liquid smoke," one of the ingredients of the recipe, may sound like something Wile E. Coyote would use to bamboozle the Roadrunner, but it's actually a way of getting smoky barbecue flavor into your food without the hassle of barbecuing. You might wonder what it is. On the bottle, it says the ingredients are "water and natural liquid smoke." Another mystery solved.

1	6-ounce can skinless, boneless salmon
1	8-ounce package cream cheese, softened to room temperature (see Mom Warning)
1	tablespoon lemon juice
2	teaspoons horseradish (see Mom Tip 1)
¼	teaspoon liquid smoke (see Mom Tip 2)
¼	teaspoon salt
⅛	teaspoon black pepper
¼	cup walnuts
2	tablespoons chopped fresh parsley
	Crackers

Drain the salmon and discard the liquid.

Combine the salmon, cream cheese, lemon juice, horseradish, liquid smoke, salt and pepper in a large bowl. Mix thoroughly, making sure the salmon is broken up into small pieces.

Place a sheet of plastic wrap or aluminum foil on the counter. Place the salmon mixture on top and, using a spoon or your hands, shape into a 6-inch log. Wrap it up, twist the ends so it will be completely sealed and refrigerate for 2 hours.

Chop the walnuts into ¼-inch pieces (see Mom Tip 3, page 291).

Combine the walnuts and chopped parsley on a large plate and mix evenly. Roll the salmon log in this mixture until it is completely covered with nuts and parsley. Transfer to a plate and serve immediately with crackers, or refrigerate, covered, until needed.

Mom Tip 1
▼

Horseradish is a root that can bring tears to your eyes. Bottled horseradish is available on the refrigerated shelves near the pickles and lunch meats.

Mom Tip 2
▼

Liquid smoke is stocked near the Worcestershire sauce.

Mom Tip 3
▼

Salmon Spread freezes well, so you can double the recipe and freeze half. Wrap it well in aluminum foil.

Mom Warning
▼

Use full-fat cream cheese, rather than the light or nonfat kind, to make sure that the spread holds together well.

Prosciutto and Melon

SERVES: 4

Serve with: Tortellini with Creamy Tomato Sauce (page 164) ▼ Preparation Time: 10-15 minutes

Cooking Time: None ▼ Rating: Very Easy

Can Prepare the Day Before: No

ANY RECIPE WITH ONLY TWO INGREDIENTS is my kind of recipe. There's no actual cooking involved, so once you have the ingredients, you just cut and paste. The only problems arise at the shopping stage.

All melons look good, but it's what's on the inside that counts (excuse me if I sound like Dear Abby). My mom has some techniques to land a good melon, but before she told me about them, I would just grab one and hope for the best. Sometimes they were ripe and sometimes they were rock-hard, but the prosciutto made up for it. Most delis carry this Italian ham. It is a little expensive, but in this case, money *can* buy happiness.

1   small or ½ large ripe honeydew melon (see Mom Tip 1)

½   pound thinly sliced prosciutto (see Mom Tip 2)

If you have a whole melon, cut it in half and scrape out and discard the seeds.

Cut the melon into long wedges that are about 1 inch thick at the base. Lay each wedge on a cutting board and, with a knife, cut off and discard the rind. Put 2 or 3 melon wedges on one side of each plate.

Divide the slices of prosciutto into 4 portions and place the portions attractively on the empty side of the plates.

Diners can cut their own pieces of melon and prosciutto and eat them together.

MOM TIP 1

▼

Honeydew melons are pale green
on the inside with a creamy white
or yellowish green rind. Sometimes
it's easy to tell when a melon is ripe:
you can smell the musky honeydew
odor, and the stem end "gives"
slightly when pressed. If I'm in
doubt—which is often—my secret
is to ask someone who works in the
produce department to pick out
a ripe one. Or I'll buy a half-melon,
which has been cut by the produce
experts. You can often ripen a
whole melon at home by letting
it sit out on the counter for a few
days, but once you cut into it,
you're stuck—it won't ripen any
further. These days, honeydew
melons are available practically
year-round, but they're at their
peak in the summer. They taste
best at room temperature
or very slightly chilled.

MOM TIP 2

▼

Prosciutto, also known as
Parma ham, is sold in delicatessens
and fancy food stores. Ask for it to
be sliced extra-thin. The secret of
good prosciutto is getting the wide
middle slices, rather than the
much smaller end slices. There
will always be some fat on each
slice, but the less, the better.
If possible, buy prosciutto the
day you plan to serve it,
because it dries out quickly.
If you buy it the day before,
keep it well wrapped.

Bruschetta

SERVES: 4-6

Serve with: Lasagna (page 172) ▼ **Preparation Time:** 20 minutes

Cooking Time: 1 minute ▼ **Rating:** Very Easy

Can Prepare the Day Before: No

BREAD BY ITSELF IS PRETTY BORING. If you serve your guests plain bread, you'll probably end up on Amnesty International's watch list. But put tomatoes and mushrooms on it, and bread becomes a great appetizer called *bruschetta* in Italian (pronounced "brew-SKET-tah"). The hardest part of bruschetta is balancing all the toppings on its way to your mouth.

1	large tomato
2	garlic cloves
¼	pound small mushrooms
3	tablespoons olive oil
	Dash salt
	Dash black pepper
½	long loaf French or Italian bread (see Mom Tip 1)
	Grated Parmesan cheese

Place a rack 3 inches from the broiling unit and preheat the broiler.

Wash the tomato and cut it into ¼-inch chunks. Peel and finely chop the garlic. Combine the tomato and garlic in a medium bowl, stir and set aside.

Wash the mushrooms, cut away and discard the bottom ¼ inch of the stems and slice them thin. Heat 1 tablespoon of the oil in a small frying pan over medium-high heat. Add the mushrooms and cook, stirring frequently, for about 2 minutes, or until they begin to soften. Remove from the heat and add to the tomato mixture. Season with the salt and pepper and set aside.

Cut the loaf into 12 equal slices. Brush each slice with a bit of the remaining olive oil. Put the bread on a cookie sheet, cut side up, and place under the broiler for about 30 seconds, or until it begins to brown. *Keep the oven door open and your eye on the bread so that it doesn't burn.*

Transfer the bread to a serving tray and spoon the tomato mixture onto the bread. Sprinkle very lightly with Parmesan cheese and serve with napkins or small plates.

MOM TIP 1

▼

If you prefer a ratio of more bread to topping, use Italian bread, which is thicker.

MOM TIP 2

▼

My brother Steve, who gave us this recipe, suggests adding a handful of Greek olives, chopped into ¼-inch pieces, to the tomato mixture.

Onion Focaccia

SERVES: 6-8

Serve with: Black Bean Lasagna (page 169)

Preparation Time: 20 minutes (using a food processor) or 30 minutes (by hand)

Waiting Time: 1½ hours ▼ Cooking Time: 20 minutes

Rating: Not So Easy ▼ Can Prepare the Day Before: No

I'D ALWAYS SEEN THE WORD *focaccia* on menus at Italian restaurants but had no idea what it was. I'm not very adventurous, so I never ordered it. My parents once had a bad experience ordering blindly from a menu in Hungary. The giggling waiter brought them either brains or pancreas, they can't remember which. So I usually stick to food I've heard of. Let me assure you, focaccia is not scary. It's just bread. But it has toppings, like a little pizza. Cooking with yeast isn't hard but requires some waiting around—but if you've got the patience, focaccia is even better than garlic bread.

1 ¼-ounce package active dry yeast (see Mom Tip 1, page 267)

About 2 cups all-purpose flour + more if needed

½ teaspoon salt

⅓ cup olive oil + more for greasing bowl

About ½ cup warm water (see Mom Warning, page 267)

TOPPING

2 medium onions

2 tablespoons olive oil + more for greasing cookie sheets

6 tablespoons crumbled feta cheese (see Mom Tip 1, page 95)

Dash salt and black pepper

2 teaspoons olive oil

With a food processor: Combine the yeast, 2 cups flour and salt in the appliance bowl. Turn on the machine and add the oil slowly through the opening at the top. While the machine is still on, gradually add enough water so the dough rolls itself into a ball. The dough should feel like soft modeling clay. You may need slightly more than ½ cup water (see Mom Tip 1). Process for 1 more minute.

By hand: Combine the yeast and ½ cup warm water in a large bowl and stir with a large wooden or plastic spoon for a few seconds, until the yeast dissolves. Add the oil, 2 cups flour and salt and stir until the ingredients are well mixed and can be formed into a rough ball (see Mom Tip 1). The dough should feel like soft modeling clay.

Sprinkle 1 tablespoon flour on a cutting board or other clean flat work surface, put the dough on the flour and knead (see Mom Tip 2) for about 5 minutes, or until the dough is smooth and stretchy. Add 1 to 2 more tablespoons flour if the dough is sticking to your hands. Shape it into a ball.

Put ½ teaspoon oil in the bottom of a large bowl and spread it around with a paper towel, making sure to oil the sides as well as the bottom. Put the dough into the bowl, cover the bowl with a tea towel or plastic wrap and set aside on the kitchen counter for 1 hour, or until the dough doubles in size (see Mom Tip 3).

MEANWHILE, MAKE THE TOPPING: Peel and finely slice the onions. Heat the oil in a medium frying pan over medium heat. Add the onions and cook for about 5 minutes, stirring occasionally, until they begin to soften. Remove from the heat and set aside.

After the dough has risen for 1 hour, lightly rub 2 cookie sheets with oil, or use nonstick sheets. Set aside.

Hit the dough with your fist to make it collapse. Cut it in half and shape each half into a ball. Roll or stretch each ball into an 8-inch circle or rectangle and place on the cookie sheets.

Put the onion slices on the dough shapes, distributing them as evenly as possible. Sprinkle on the cheese, salt and pepper. Drizzle 1 teaspoon oil over each. Set aside for 30 minutes to let rise.

About 15 minutes before baking, place one oven rack in the top position and the other in the bottom position. Preheat the oven to 400 degrees.

Bake for about 20 minutes, or until the focaccia begins to brown. Remove from the oven and cut into quarters or eighths. Transfer to a plate and serve immediately.

MOM TIP 1

▼

If the dough won't stick together, add 1 to 2 more tablespoons warm water. If the dough is so sticky it clings to your hands, add 1 to 2 more tablespoons flour, or even more if necessary.

MOM TIP 2

▼

Kneading means folding and pushing the dough with your hands so that it becomes smooth and will eventually rise.

MOM TIP 3

▼

For yeast dough to rise successfully, it should be covered to keep out drafts and left in a warm place. Some people advise putting the bowl in an unheated oven, keeping the heat off. I did that once and forgot about it for several hours. Luckily, no harm was done. Yeast dough is very forgiving.

 SOUPS

SOUP IS A VERY COMFORTING FOOD. When people are sick, they eat chicken soup. But unless you're catering for a hospital ward, you need something a little more exciting for your friends. Who's to say Leek and Potato Soup doesn't pep you up? Maybe Tortilla Soup cures tired blood. I'll compile all my theories in my next book, *Borscht for the Soul.*

At restaurants, soup is often treated as the liquid equivalent of breadsticks. It's just another filler on the way to the entrée. When I make soups for company, I like them to be the hearty kind that can be either an appetizer or a main dish. The great thing about all these soups is that you can turn them from appetizers into main courses simply by using bigger bowls.

▲

Recipes

▼

Creamy Mushroom Soup

SERVES: 4

Serve with: Crunchy Baked Fish (page 252) ▼ Preparation Time: 15 minutes

Cooking Time: 15 minutes ▼ Rating: Very Easy ▼ Can Prepare the Day Before: Yes

WHEN ASKED IF HE CARES FOR MUSHROOMS, my friend Scott defiantly declares, "I shall eat no fungus!" That's a little inflammatory. While mushrooms are part of the fungus family, they can rise above their station. Don't listen to Scott. He prefers foods invented in this century, like cheese that comes out of aerosol cans.

Homemade mushroom soup is the best way to eat mushrooms. It's not like the canned version, where the mushrooms taste like soft rubber. This recipe has been pleasing members of my family for three generations.

1	pound mushrooms
1	small onion
1	garlic clove
1	tablespoon butter or margarine
1	tablespoon olive oil
1	tablespoon all-purpose flour
1/8	teaspoon ground nutmeg
	Dash black pepper
2	10½-ounce cans condensed chicken broth + 2 cans water
	(or 2 vegetable bouillon cubes + 5 cups water)
½	cup whipping (not whipped) cream

Wash the mushrooms, cut away and discard the bottom ¼ inch of the stems. Cut the mushrooms in half. Peel and finely slice the onion. Peel and finely chop the garlic.

Heat the butter or margarine and olive oil in a medium pot over medium heat. Add the mushrooms, onion and garlic and cook for about 5 minutes, stirring occasionally, until the vegetables begin to soften. The mushrooms will shrink a lot.

Add the flour and stir carefully until it is fully absorbed into the vegetable mixture. Add the nutmeg, pepper and chicken broth (or vegetable cubes) and water. Bring the mixture to a boil over high heat. Turn down the heat to low, cover and cook for 10 minutes. The vegetables will be very soft. Remove the soup from the heat.

With a blender or food processor: Transfer the cooked vegetables and liquid to the appliance bowl (see Mom Tip). Blend at high speed for about 20 seconds, or until the mixture is smooth. Return the soup to the pot.

By hand: Skip to the next step. The soup will be chunky rather than smooth.

Stir the cream into the soup. Reheat over medium-high heat until the soup is hot but not boiling. Serve immediately.

Mom Tip

▼

A blender is particularly useful for making smooth soups.
It grinds up cooked vegetables and broth within seconds.
Many food processors leak when filled beyond a certain
point; if yours does, make the soup in batches.

Leek and Potato Soup

SERVES: 4

Serve with: Chicken with Red Wine (page 228) ▼ Preparation Time: 25 minutes

Cooking Time: 25 minutes ▼ Rating: Easy ▼ Can Prepare the Day Before: Yes

LEEKS ARE ONE OF YOUR STRANGER VEGETABLES. To the uninitiated, they look like scallions from *The Land That Time Forgot*. But they eat better than they look. I grew up on this soup, and I made sure it was put in the book.

You really need to have a blender or food processor to make this soup. If you don't have one, it's time to get married. No married couple fails to get three or more blending devices as gifts. Species mutate faster than it would take to puree leeks by hand.

 2   leeks (about 1 pound; see Mom Tip 1)
 2   tablespoons olive oil
2-3   medium potatoes (see Mom Tip 2)
 1   10½-ounce can condensed chicken broth + 2 cans water
        (or 1 vegetable bouillon cube + 4 cups water)
 ½   teaspoon salt
 ¼   teaspoon black pepper
 ½   cup whipping (not whipped) cream (optional)

Wash the leeks as thoroughly as you can. Cut off the root tip and the top 4 inches of the green parts and discard them. Cut the remaining white and green parts into ½-inch slices.

Heat the oil in a medium pot over medium-high heat. When it is hot, add the leeks. Cover and cook for about 5 minutes until they begin to soften.

Meanwhile, peel the potatoes and cut them into ¼-inch-thick slices.

Add the potatoes, chicken broth (or vegetable cube) and water, salt and pepper to the pot and bring the mixture to a boil over high heat. Turn down the heat to low, cover and cook for about 20 minutes, or until the potatoes are very soft and can easily be pierced with a fork. Remove the soup from the heat.

With a blender or food processor: Transfer the cooked vegetables and liquid to the appliance bowl (see Mom Tip, page 69). Blend at high speed for about 20 seconds, or until the mixture is smooth. Depending on the size of your equipment, you may have to do this in batches. Return the soup to the pot.

By hand: Mash the potatoes with the back of a spoon. The soup will be chunky rather than smooth. If desired, stir the cream into the soup. Reheat over medium-high heat until the soup is hot but not boiling. Serve immediately.

MOM TIP 1
▼

Leeks look like large scallions. They are sold loose or in bundles of two or three in the vegetable department. Choose leeks that have as much white part as possible. Getting the dirt off leeks can be challenging. The best way I've found is to cut the leek lengthwise in half and rinse both sides of the layers under cold running water. Most of the dirt is between the green layers, especially where the green meets the white.

MOM TIP 2
▼

This soup will vary in flavor, texture and color depending on the number of potatoes you use. Fewer potatoes mean the soup will be thinner and greener. Extra potatoes will make it very hearty and more filling but slightly bland. Add more water to make it thinner.

MOM TIP 3
▼

When served cold, with the cream, Leek and Potato Soup is called Vichyssoise.

Minestrone

SERVES: 4

Serve with: Penne Arrabbiata (page 162) ▼ Preparation Time: 20 minutes

Cooking Time: 35 minutes ▼ Rating: Easy ▼ Can Prepare the Day Before: Yes

My wife Jody and I were at one of those 24-hour diners in Las Vegas. We had just spent two hours waiting for the third Lucky 7 to make an appearance on a slot machine, and we wanted something warm to keep our spirits up. We asked the waiter what the "Soup du Jour" was. He replied, "That is the soup of the day." I guess that's what you should expect at 3 A.M. He eventually brought back some Minestrone, which seems to be the soup of the day wherever I go. Your guests will appreciate our taste-filled Minestrone, which hasn't been sitting over low heat for the last 14 hours.

1	large onion
1	large carrot
1	large celery stalk
1	large zucchini
¼	pound fresh green beans
⅛	large cabbage (about 1 cup shredded; see Mom Tip 1)
2	tablespoons olive oil
1	15-ounce can black beans (see Mom Tip 2)
1	15-ounce can ready-cut tomatoes
1	10½-ounce can condensed beef broth + 1 can water
	(or 1 vegetable bouillon cube + 3 cups water)
½	teaspoon dried thyme
½	teaspoon dried basil
¼	teaspoon black pepper

¼ cup uncooked small pasta (such as elbow macaroni,
   salad macaroni or small shells)
Grated Parmesan cheese

Peel the onion and carrot and cut them into ¼-inch pieces. Wash the celery and zucchini, trim and discard the ends and cut into ¼-inch slices. Wash the green beans. Snap ¼ inch off each end of each bean and pull; if a string comes off, throw it away with the ends. Cut the beans into ½-inch lengths. Cut the cabbage into ½-inch-wide shreds. Set aside.

Heat the oil in a large pot over medium heat. Add the onion, carrot and celery pieces and cook for about 5 minutes, stirring occasionally, until the vegetables begin to soften.

While they are cooking, drain the black beans, discarding the liquid, and rinse them in a strainer or colander under cold running water.

Add the black beans, tomatoes and their liquid, beef broth (or vegetable bouillon cube) and water, thyme, basil and pepper to the pot and bring to a boil over high heat. Turn down the heat to medium, cover and cook for 15 minutes.

Add the zucchini, green beans, cabbage and pasta, cover and continue cooking for another 15 minutes, or until the pasta is soft. Serve with Parmesan cheese.

MOM TIP 1

▼

Several types of cabbage are usually available.
Green cabbage is very pale green and compact; at
first glance, it looks like iceberg lettuce. Red cabbage
is actually deep purple and is also compact. Savoy
cabbage is darker green with looser leaves. Any one
of these is appropriate. However, do not choose
Chinese cabbage, which is oval-shaped and has a
celery-stalk-like base and delicate, crinkly,
pale green leaves.

MOM TIP 2

▼

Kidney, pinto or white beans
can easily be substituted.

MOM WARNING

▼

This soup doesn't need any extra salt because
there's plenty of salt already in the broth,
tomatoes and black beans.

Russian Vegetable Borscht

SERVES: 4

Serve with: Chicken Kiev (page 237) ▼ Preparation Time: 20-25 minutes

Cooking Time: 45 minutes ▼ Rating: Easy

Can Prepare the Day Before: Yes

WHEN I FIRST BOUGHT BEETS, the checkout lady grimaced when she had to touch them. That's because beets look less like food than something you'd hire people to remove from the backyard. And they squirt a permanent purple dye when you cut into them. But once the beet has been tamed, it's easy to see how Russians have survived on borscht for centuries. You can also use canned beets and avoid all the hassle.

1	large carrot
1	medium onion
2	medium fresh beets (see Mom Tip 1) or one 15-ounce can shoestring beets
2½	cups water
¼	large cabbage (about 2 cups shredded; see Mom Tip 1, page 73) or half a 16-ounce package shredded cabbage
3	tablespoons ketchup
2	tablespoons red wine vinegar
1	tablespoon sugar
1	bay leaf
½	teaspoon salt
⅛	teaspoon black pepper
¼	cup sour cream (optional)

Peel the carrot, onion and beets, if using fresh beets. Cut or shred the carrot and beets lengthwise into ⅛-inch-thick 1-inch-long matchsticks (see Mom Tip 2 and Mom Warning). Cut the onion in half and slice it into ⅛-inch-thick slices. If you are using canned beets, drain the liquid into a container and set the beets and liquid aside.

Put the carrots, onion and fresh beets in a large pot (do not add canned beets). Add 1 cup of the water and bring the mixture to a boil over high heat. Turn down the heat to medium-low, cover and cook for 15 minutes.

Meanwhile, cut or shred the cabbage into ⅛-inch-thick slices.

When the soup has cooked for 15 minutes, add the remaining 1½ cups water, the cabbage, ketchup, vinegar, sugar, bay leaf, salt, pepper and the canned beets, if using (do not add the canned beet liquid). Bring the mixture back to a boil over high heat. Turn down the heat to medium-low, cover and cook for 30 minutes. The vegetables will be very soft.

Add the beet liquid—it will turn the soup beet-red—and heat through. Remove from the heat and remove and discard the bay leaf. If desired, serve with a tablespoon of sour cream on top of each bowl; or offer the sour cream in a separate bowl.

MOM TIP 1

▼

Fresh beets are usually available in the vegetable department. They are a root vegetable, like carrots, and are often sold 3 or 4 to a bundle, with their long stems still attached. They look like egg-size radishes. Remove and discard the stems before preparing as above.

MOM TIP 2

▼

If you have a food processor with a shredding attachment, use it to cut up all the vegetables. It will make the job much quicker. You can also use a grater, although not for the onions, or you will be very tearful.

MOM WARNING

▼

Beet juice may temporarily stain a wooden cutting board, as well as your fingers. Be careful not to get it on your clothes.

Black Bean Soup

SERVES: 4

Serve with: Ratatouille (page 182)

Preparation Time: 15 minutes (using a blender or food processor) or 20 minutes (by hand)

Cooking Time: 25 minutes ▼ Rating: Easy ▼ Can Prepare the Day Before: Yes

BACK WHEN MY PARENTS HAD RECENTLY BEEN MARRIED, Dad requested that Mom make this soup, which his mom had made for him when he was growing up. If my mom had been more like me, she would have said, "Make it yourself." But she obliged him. When Grandma was coy about her recipe, Mom pieced the ingredients together from eyewitness accounts and expert testimony. The end result was even better than Dad remembered. Recently, Grandma came clean: she got the soup out of a can. Say it ain't so, Grandma.

1 large or 2 small carrots

1 medium onion

4 garlic cloves

8 sprigs fresh cilantro; see Mom Tip (optional)

2 tablespoons corn oil or olive oil

2 15-ounce cans black beans (see Mom Warning)

2 teaspoons curry powder

1 teaspoon ground coriander

½ teaspoon black pepper

1 vegetable bouillon cube + 3 cups water

2 tablespoons lemon juice

Peel the carrot(s) and onion and thinly slice them. Peel and finely chop the garlic. Wash the cilantro sprigs, if using, and pat them dry between paper towels. Cut off and discard the stems and cut the leafy parts into ½-inch pieces.

Heat the oil in a medium pot over medium heat. Add the carrots, onion, garlic and cilantro and cook for about 5 minutes, stirring occasionally, until the vegetables begin to soften.

While they are cooking, drain the beans, discarding the liquid, and rinse them in a strainer or colander under cold running water. Set aside.

Add the curry powder, coriander and pepper to the vegetables and stir. When they've been incorporated, add the beans, vegetable bouillon cube and water. Bring to a boil, cover, turn down the heat to medium-low and cook for 20 minutes. Remove from the heat.

Strain out half the beans and vegetables using a slotted spoon and process in a blender or food processor until they become a thick sauce, about 30 seconds. Or put them in a bowl and mash them as fine as possible with a fork. Return this sauce to the soup and stir thoroughly to thicken the soup. Reheat the soup. When it is hot, add the lemon juice, stir and serve.

MOM TIP

▼

Like parsley, fresh cilantro is sold
in bunches. It has a distinctive flavor
that works well in Mexican dishes.

MOM WARNING

▼

Any canned beans, except those
that come in a sauce, should be
drained and then rinsed in a strainer
or colander to remove excess salt.

Boston Clam Chowder

SERVES: 4

Serve with: Stuffed Peppers (page 186)   ▼   Preparation Time: 15 minutes

Cooking Time: 35 minutes   ▼   Rating: Easy   ▼   Can Prepare the Day Before: Yes

THERE ARE THREE RIVALRIES between Boston and New York: the Red Sox/Yankees, the Celtics/Knicks and clam chowder. The Boston version uses cream and bacon, the Manhattan uses tomatoes. In my opinion, their sports teams can be left to drown in their respective harbors. But when it comes to clam chowder, I'm on Boston's side, at least until Los Angeles comes up with its own version, flavored with wheatgrass juice.

4   slices bacon

1   medium onion

3   medium potatoes

2   6½-ounce cans chopped or minced clams (see Mom Tip)

2   cups water

1   cup milk

1   cup whipping (not whipped) cream

2   tablespoons butter or margarine

¼   teaspoon salt

¼   teaspoon black pepper

Put the bacon in a large frying pan and begin cooking over medium-high heat. As it cooks, it will begin to shrink. After 4 to 5 minutes, drain off the fat into an empty can. After the bacon browns on one side, turn it over, turn down the heat to medium so that it doesn't burn and cook until it gets crisp, about 5 more minutes.

Remove from the heat, transfer the bacon to paper towels to drain and pat it with another paper towel to absorb extra grease. Save 1 tablespoon of the bacon fat and discard the rest. Break or cut the bacon into 1-inch pieces and set aside.

Peel the onion and cut it into ½-inch pieces. Peel the potatoes and cut them into ½-inch pieces.

Add the bacon fat to a medium pot and begin heating over medium heat. Add the onion and cook for about 5 minutes, stirring occasionally, until it begins to soften. Add the potatoes, the juice only from the cans of clams and the water and bring to a boil over high heat. Turn down the heat to medium, cover and cook for about 20 minutes, or until the potatoes are soft.

Add the milk, cream, butter or margarine, clams, bacon pieces, salt and pepper and continue cooking just until the butter or margarine melts. Stir and serve.

MOM TIP

▼

If you happen to live in New England or other areas
where fresh clams are readily available, you may prefer to use
them rather than the canned variety. Buy hard-shelled
clams (you will need about 1 quart), either quahogs
(the largest and cheapest) or cherrystones (smaller, more
expensive and more tender). To prepare fresh clams, scrub
the shells to remove sand or other debris, put them
in a large pot with 2 cups water and cook, covered,
over high heat for about 5 minutes, or until all the shells
have opened. If any of the clams do not open, discard them.
When cool, remove the clams from their shells and
cut them into ¼-inch pieces. Strain the broth and
use it instead of the water called for in the recipe.
Many stores also sell minced fresh clams.

Chinese Chicken and Corn Soup

SERVES: 4

Serve with: Pasta with Mushrooms and Artichokes (page 160) ▼ Preparation Time: 10 minutes

Cooking Time: 10 minutes ▼ Rating: Easy

Can Prepare the Day Before: Yes

FOR THOSE WHO ARE TIRED of the standard Chinese takeout food, here's an alternative. This soup is a substantial meal, and it won't leave you hungry soon after you're finished. You don't want your guests poking around the fridge a half hour after dinner.

1	scallion
1	10½-ounce can condensed chicken broth + 2 cans water
1	15-ounce can cream-style corn
1	teaspoon sesame oil (see Mom Tip 1, page 143)
½	teaspoon ground ginger
	Dash salt
	Dash black pepper
½	pound ground chicken or turkey (see Mom Tip)
1	tablespoon cornstarch or 2 tablespoons all-purpose flour
2	tablespoons cold water
1	large egg

Wash the scallion. Cut off the root tip and top 2 inches of the green part and discard them. Cut the remaining white and green parts into ¼-inch pieces and set aside.

Combine the chicken broth and water, corn, sesame oil, ginger, salt and pepper in a large pot and heat over high heat. When it comes to a boil, add the chicken or turkey, breaking it into marble-size clumps with a spoon. Turn down the heat to medium, cover and let the soup cook for about 3 minutes, or until the meat turns white.

Meanwhile, mix the cornstarch or flour and cold water together in a cup and stir well; if using cornstarch, make sure it is dissolved (see Mom Warning, page 230).

Add the cornstarch or flour mixture to the soup, turn up the heat to medium-high and stir until it has come to a boil again and becomes slightly thicker.

Beat the egg in a small dish. Pour the egg slowly through the tines of a fork into the soup and stir. The egg will cook immediately and separate into tiny shreds. Add the scallion pieces and remove from the heat. Stir and serve.

Mom Tip

▼

Fresh ground chicken and turkey are usually available
at the meat counter. Frozen 1-pound packages of ground
chicken and ground turkey may also be available in the
frozen food section. Since this recipe calls for
only ½ pound, you have two options on what
to do with the extra ½ pound:

▼ Double the recipe.

▼ Make Asian Turkey Burgers with Ginger Soy Sauce
(page 240).

Tortilla Soup

SERVES: 4

Serve with: Mexican Grilled Cornish Hens (page 224)

Preparation Time: 15 minutes ▼ Cooking Time: 15 minutes ▼ Rating: Easy

Can Prepare the Day Before: Partially (but don't add the avocado, tortilla chips and cheese until just before serving)

THIS IS A SOUP I discovered at one of my favorite restaurants. It seemed odd to me that it was called Tortilla Soup when it was mostly tomato soup. But it tasted good, so I didn't question it. The tortilla chips serve the same basic function as saltines do in other soups, providing a little something to chew on. So how come there's nothing called saltine soup?

Some recipes for Tortilla Soup tell you to make your own tortillas. That sounds like a lot of extra work. My Uncle Saul makes his own. But store-bought tortilla chips work just fine for me, and no one has ever complained that they weren't up to snuff.

1	medium onion
3	garlic cloves
8	sprigs fresh cilantro
2	tablespoons corn oil or olive oil
1	bay leaf
1	teaspoon ground cumin
1	teaspoon chili powder
	Dash cayenne pepper
1	8-ounce can tomato sauce
2	10½-ounce cans condensed chicken broth + 2 cans water
	(or 2 vegetable bouillon cubes + 5 cups water)
1	ripe avocado (see Mom Tip 1)

1   **cooked chicken breast or leftover cooked chicken (optional)**

20   **tortilla chips**

½   **cup shredded cheddar or Monterey Jack cheese**

Peel and finely chop the onion and garlic (see Mom Tip 2). Wash the cilantro sprigs and pat them dry between paper towels. Cut off and discard the stems and cut the leafy parts into ½-inch pieces.

Heat the oil in a medium pot over medium heat. Add the onion, garlic and cilantro and cook for about 5 minutes, stirring occasionally, until the vegetables begin to soften.

Add the bay leaf, cumin, chili powder and cayenne pepper and stir briefly so that the spices are absorbed by the oil (see Mom Tip 3). Add the tomato sauce and chicken broth (or vegetable cubes) and water. Bring the mixture to a boil over high heat. Turn down the heat to low, cover and cook for 10 minutes.

While the soup is cooking, cut the avocado lengthwise the whole way around and twist to separate the halves. Cover and refrigerate the half with the pit for use in another recipe, such as Broccoli, Avocado and Tomato Salad (page 98). Peel the remaining half and cut it into ¼-inch pieces. Set aside.

If you are including chicken in the soup, cut it into bite-size pieces and set aside.

When you are ready to serve the soup, remove and discard the bay leaf. Pour the soup into 4 bowls, filling them three-fourths full. Distribute the avocado and chicken pieces, if using, and tortilla chips equally among the bowls and top with the cheese. Serve immediately.

MOM TIP 1
▼

Ripe avocados "give" slightly when you press them; unripe avocados are hard. Another clue: the skin of ripe avocados is a darker green than that of unripe ones. Once you cut into an avocado, it will not ripen any further.

MOM TIP 2
▼

A blender or food processor allows you to chop onions and garlic very quickly. A mini food processor is also good for this task.

MOM TIP 3
▼

Spices are absorbed better and their flavor is stronger when they are added to hot oil.

Mexican Meatball Soup

SERVES: 4 AS A MEAL, 8 AS A SOUP

Serve with: Corn Bread (page 132) ▼ Preparation Time: 30 minutes

Cooking Time: 25 minutes ▼ Rating: Not So Easy ▼ Can Prepare the Day Before: Yes

I LIKE THE CONCEPT OF THE ONE-DISH MEAL. In this soup, you've got your vegetables, you've got your meat and you've got your rice, all under one lid. This fits into my philosophy of keeping hassles to a minimum. One bowl, one spoon, one full stomach.

MEATBALLS

1 garlic clove

½ cup fresh cilantro sprigs (about 40)

1 pound lean ground beef (see Mom Tip 1)

1 large egg

¾ cup cooked rice or ¼ cup uncooked rice; see Mom Tip 2 (optional)

1 teaspoon ground cumin

¼ teaspoon black pepper

SOUP

1 medium onion

2 large celery stalks

2 tablespoons olive oil

1 medium zucchini

2 10½-ounce cans condensed chicken broth + 2 cans water

1 15-ounce can ready-cut tomatoes

1 teaspoon dried oregano

½   teaspoon ground coriander

½   teaspoon black pepper

MEATBALLS: Peel and finely chop the garlic. Wash the cilantro sprigs and pat them dry between paper towels. Cut off and discard the stems and cut the leafy parts into ¼-inch pieces.

Combine the garlic, cilantro, ground beef, egg, cooked rice (if using), cumin and pepper in a large bowl and mix thoroughly with a fork or your hands. Shape the mixture into 1-inch balls and set aside on a plate.

SOUP: Peel the onion and cut it in ½-inch pieces. Wash the celery stalks, trim off and discard the ends and cut the stalks into ¼-inch slices.

Heat the oil in a large pot over medium heat. Add the onion and celery pieces and cook for about 5 minutes, stirring occasionally, until the vegetables begin to soften.

Meanwhile, wash the zucchini, cut off and discard the ends and cut into ¼-inch cubes. Set aside.

Add the chicken broth and water, tomatoes and their liquid, oregano, coriander and pepper to the pot and bring to a boil over high heat. Add the meatballs. When the mixture returns to a boil, turn down the heat to medium, cover and cook for 10 minutes (see Mom Warning). Add the zucchini and continue cooking, covered, for another 5 minutes. Stir and serve.

MOM TIP 1
▼

The leaner the ground beef, the better. The meatballs cook right in the soup, so there is no way to drain the fat. Ground turkey or ground chicken can be substituted for ground beef.

MOM TIP 2
▼

If you don't have any leftover rice, cook some as follows: Pour ½ cup water into a small pot, cover and bring to a boil. Add ¼ cup rice, return to a boil, stir, cover and turn the heat to low. Cook for 15 minutes and then remove from the heat.

MOM WARNING
▼

If you like golf-ball-size meatballs, cook the soup for an extra 10 minutes before adding the zucchini.

Untraditional Matzo Ball Soup

SERVES: 4

Serve with: Hungarian Goulash (page 194) ▼ Preparation Time: 25 minutes

Cooking Time: 40 minutes ▼ Rating: Not So Easy ▼ Can Prepare the Day Before: Yes

IF YOU'VE NEVER HAD MATZO BALL SOUP, you probably have no idea what matzo balls are. As one Jewish friend described them to her gentile fiancé, they're "light, fluffy dumplings." This is a traditional Jewish dish, and many Jewish people, including my father-in-law, will drive for miles searching for the matzo ball soup of their youth.

Traditionally, it's just matzo balls and chicken broth. Our version keeps those traditional elements but adds vegetables and spices. Is that blasphemy? No, because my father-in-law asked for the recipe. If your guests are purists, their views will soften once they taste it. If they've never had matzo ball soup before, they won't know any better.

MATZO BALLS

½ cup matzo meal (see Mom Tip 1)

1 teaspoon salt

2 large eggs

2 tablespoons water

2 tablespoons corn oil or vegetable oil

SOUP

1 medium onion

1 medium celery stalk

1 medium carrot

2 garlic cloves

2	tablespoons olive oil
1	cup canned ready-cut tomatoes
2	10½-ounce cans condensed chicken broth + 2 cans water
	(or 2 vegetable bouillon cubes + 5 cups water)
1	teaspoon chopped fresh dill or ½ teaspoon dried (see Mom Tips 2 and 3)
¼	teaspoon black pepper

MATZO BALLS: Combine the matzo meal, salt, eggs, water and oil in a medium bowl. Stir vigorously with a fork until well mixed. Cover and refrigerate for at least 15 minutes, or until needed. Begin making the soup.

SOUP: Peel the onion and cut it into ½-inch pieces. Wash the celery stalk. Trim off and discard the ends and cut it into ¼-inch slices. Peel the carrot and cut it into ¼-inch pieces. Peel and finely chop the garlic.

Heat the oil in a large pot over medium heat. Add the onion, celery, carrot and garlic and cook for about 5 minutes, stirring occasionally, until the vegetables begin to soften. Add the tomatoes and their liquid, chicken broth (or vegetable cubes) and water, dill and pepper and let cook while you make the matzo balls.

Remove the matzo ball mixture from the refrigerator. Divide it into 8 portions, forming each portion into a small ball with a spoon or an ice cream scoop. The mixture will be very sticky.

Drop the matzo balls into the soup one at a time, making sure they don't stick to each other. Stir gently. Cover the pot and cook over medium-low heat for about 35 minutes, or until the matzo balls have doubled in size and are fully cooked (see Mom Warning). Serve hot.

Mom Tip 1

▼

Matzo meal is available in 12-ounce boxes in the Jewish food section of the supermarket.

Mom Tip 2

▼

Fresh dill is usually available in plastic packages or sometimes in bunches, like parsley, in the vegetable department. Wash it and pat it dry between paper towels. Then cut or snip the leafy parts into ¼-inch lengths and discard the thick stems. Leftover dill sprigs will keep for about 1 week in the refrigerator. Or they can be wrapped in plastic and frozen for future use.

Mom Tip 3

▼

To give the soup an Italian flavor, add ¼ cup chopped fresh parsley (or 2 teaspoons dried), 1 bay leaf, 1 teaspoon dried oregano and ½ teaspoon dried basil in place of the dill.

Mom Warning

▼

Matzo balls that are not fully cooked in the middle are heavy. The only way to tell if they are done is to remove one from the pot and cut it in half. The center should be about the same color and texture as the edges. If it's much darker and denser, the matzo balls need to be cooked for another 5 to 10 minutes.

SALADS / SALAD DRESSINGS

WHEN I'M AT A RESTAURANT, I can usually tell how good the meal is going to be by the quality of the salad. If it's just hacked-up lettuce and a few limp pieces of tomato, I know I'll still be hungry when I get home. But if the salad I'm served has some personality, maybe a worm or two, I'm already looking forward to the next course. So when I prepare a salad, I make sure that it's more than just rabbit food.

There seems to be debate about when in the meal to serve the salad. Do you serve it before, during or after the main course? My answer is, who cares? Different families do it different ways. My advice is to put the salad on the table at the beginning and let your guests figure out when they want to eat it. My dad waits until the end of the meal and then eats all the salad that's left.

My friends are just as impressed that I make my own dressing as they would be if I told them that I churned my own butter. But the truth is, I wouldn't do it if it weren't virtually as easy as opening a bottle.

▲

Recipes

▼

Caesar Salad

SERVES: 4-6

Serve with: Mexican Grilled Cornish Hens (page 224) ▼ Preparation Time: 20 minutes

Cooking Time: None ▼ Rating: Easy ▼ Can Prepare the Day Before: No

I HAD ALWAYS ASSUMED this salad was named after Julius Caesar. I thought that when he wasn't conquering the Gauls and solidifying his power in Rome, perhaps he was in the kitchen subduing the lettuce and the anchovies. But actually, this salad was invented in the 1920s in Mexico. So much for truth in advertising.

1	large head romaine lettuce (see Mom Tip 1)
4-6	anchovy fillets (see Mom Tip 2)
1	garlic clove
3	tablespoons lemon juice
½	cup olive oil
¼	cup flaked or grated Parmesan cheese (see Mom Tip 3)
½-1	cup packaged croutons
	Dash black pepper

Separate the lettuce leaves, wash them and pat them dry with paper towels. Tear into bite-size pieces and transfer to a large salad bowl. Cut the anchovies into ¼-inch pieces and add them to the bowl.

Peel and finely chop the garlic. Combine the garlic, lemon juice and olive oil in a jar or plastic container with a tightly closing lid. Shake until the ingredients are thoroughly combined and pour over the salad.

Add the Parmesan cheese, croutons and pepper, toss and serve immediately. If the salad sits around very long, the croutons get soggy.

Mom Tip 1

▼

Romaine lettuce has long leaves, which you snap off from a stalky base. It has more flavor than iceberg or leaf lettuce.

Mom Tip 2

▼

Anchovies are tiny fish packed in small cans, which can be found near the canned tuna. They are very salty and have a strong flavor, so use them sparingly—unless you're like me and love anchovies. I use the whole can in my Caesar Salad. Ground anchovies are also available in tubes like toothpaste: ½ teaspoon anchovy paste equals 1 anchovy. Add the paste to the dressing and shake until thoroughly mixed.

Mom Tip 3

▼

Instead of using the Parmesan cheese in green plastic containers, buy a chunk of Parmesan cheese (found in the cheese department of many grocery stores); the flavor will be much better. With a potato peeler, slice some of it into paper-thin flakes about ½ inch wide and 1 inch long and scatter over the salad, or grate it, using the largest holes on your grater. Or if you prefer traditional grated Parmesan cheese, grate it on the smallest holes of your grater. Put the extra cheese in a plastic storage bag or wrap tightly in plastic wrap and refrigerate.

Mom Warning

▼

Traditionally, a raw egg is used in this dressing. However, with the current concern about salmonella contaminating eggs, I've decided to eliminate the egg. The taste of the salad dressing is slightly different but it's still better than most restaurant Caesar salads— at least the ones I've had lately.

Greek Salad

SERVES: 4 AS A MAIN COURSE, 8 AS A SALAD

Serve with: Grilled Salmon (page 250) ▼ Preparation Time: 20 minutes

Cooking Time: None ▼ Rating: Easy ▼ Can Prepare the Day Before: No

THERE ARE TWO ACQUIRED TASTES in Greek salad. The first, feta cheese, used to make me cry. It has a salty, slightly bitter taste, and as a kid, I couldn't believe adults ate it voluntarily. Over the years, though, feta cheese has grown on me.

The other taste that has its enemies is olives. It's been said that in every couple, one person will love them and the other will hate them. Luckily for me, Greek salad tastes just as good without the olives or, as my wife believes, with twice the olives.

1	small head romaine lettuce (see Mom Tip 1, page 93)
3	large tomatoes
1	medium cucumber
¼	medium red onion
4	ounces crumbled feta cheese (see Mom Tip 1)
12	black olives; see Mom Tip 2 (optional)

DRESSING

2	garlic cloves
½	cup olive oil
3	tablespoons red wine vinegar
2	tablespoons lemon juice
1	teaspoon dried oregano
1	teaspoon salt

¼ teaspoon dried dill

⅛ teaspoon black pepper

Separate the lettuce leaves, wash them and pat them dry with paper towels. Tear into bite-size pieces and put in a large salad bowl.

Wash the tomatoes and cut them into bite-size pieces. Peel the cucumber and slice lengthwise in half. Scrape out and discard the seeds and cut into ¼-inch slices. Thinly slice the onion and cut the slices into 1-inch pieces. Add these ingredients to the salad bowl.

Sprinkle the cheese on top. Add the olives.

DRESSING: Peel and finely chop the garlic. Combine the garlic, olive oil, vinegar, lemon juice, oregano, salt, dill and pepper in a jar or plastic container with a tightly closing lid. Shake until the ingredients are thoroughly combined.

Pour the dressing over the salad and toss. Serve immediately, or refrigerate, covered, until needed.

MOM TIP 1

▼

Packages of crumbled feta cheese
are usually available in the refrigerated
cheese section. Some crumbled
feta cheeses have herbs added,
and these are particularly
suited to Greek salad.

MOM TIP 2

▼

Buy black olives at the deli counter.
They're much more flavorful
than bland canned black olives.
Kalamatas from Greece are the
usual choice for this salad,
but you can use any variety.

Spinach and Strawberry Salad

SERVES: 4

Serve with: Grilled Leg of Lamb (page 206) ▼ **Preparation Time:** 10-15 minutes

Cooking Time: None ▼ **Rating:** Very Easy (if you use prewashed spinach)

Can Prepare the Day Before: No

STRAWBERRIES AND SPINACH sounds like a mistake ("Hey, you got your spinach in my strawberries!"). But it turns out that combining strawberries and spinach doesn't double the taste. It increases it to the power of two.

1 basket strawberries (about 12 strawberries; see Mom Warning)
4 loosely packed cups (about 3 ounces) small fresh spinach leaves
   (see Mom Tip 1)
2 scallions
   Vinaigrette dressing (see Mom Tip 2)
¼ cup slivered almonds (see Mom Tip 3)

Rinse the strawberries and remove and discard the stems. Cut them lengthwise into ⅛-inch-thick slices and put them in a large salad bowl. Wash and dry the spinach if it's not already been washed. If the stems are very long, remove and discard them. Add the spinach to the salad bowl.

Wash the scallions. Cut off the root tip and top 2 inches of the green parts and discard them. Cut the remaining white and green parts into ¼-inch pieces and add them to the bowl.

Drizzle with dressing, add the almonds, toss and serve.

Mom Warning

▼

If you buy strawberries in prepacked boxes or baskets, occasionally the berries on the bottom are crushed, have soft spots or, worst of all, have white mold growing on them. So always check the bottom of the container before buying.

Discard less-than-perfect strawberries. Also avoid strawberries with flesh that's partly white; this means they aren't fully ripe. Try to buy strawberries the day you use them; if you have to keep them overnight, store them in the refrigerator.

Mom Tip 1

▼

Buying a bag of prewashed fresh spinach is much easier than washing it yourself. However, if you buy a bundle of fresh spinach that looks as if it's just been pulled from the garden—roots, dirt and all—choose one with small flat leaves. Submerge it in cold water and swish it around to loosen the dirt. Then rinse the leaves under cold water and remove and discard any long stems. Tear any large spinach leaves into bite-size pieces.

Mom Tip 2

▼

When my friend Mary Morigaki gave me this recipe, she recommended Briannas Home Style Blush Wine Vinaigrette Dressing, found in grocery stores, either with the other salad dressings or in the gourmet food aisle. She was right. It perfectly complements this salad. Simple French Dressing (page 110) is good with it too.

Mom Tip 3

▼

Slivered almonds are available in small bags near the chocolate chips.

Broccoli, Avocado and Tomato Salad

SERVES: 4

Serve with: Mushroom Turnover (page 178) ▼ Preparation Time: 15 minutes

Cooking Time: 5 minutes ▼ Rating: Very Easy ▼ Can Prepare the Day Before: No

IF YOU HAVE ONE VEGETABLE, you have a side dish. Two or more, and you have a salad. My mom discovered this principle by accident when she combined three of her favorite vegetables. It's not as significant as the accidental discovery of penicillin, but it's a worthy advance in the field of salad making. It's nice to have a salad without lettuce once in a while.

1	large stalk broccoli (about ½ pound)
½	cup water
2	ripe avocados (see Mom Tip 1, page 83)
1	small red onion (see Mom Tip 1, page 101)
2	medium tomatoes (see Mom Warning)
	Dash salt
	Dash black pepper
	Easy Italian Dressing (page 109)

Rinse the broccoli. Trim off and discard any leaves and the bottom 1 inch of the stem. Peel off and discard ¼ inch of the tough outer surface of the stem. Slice the remaining stem into ¼-inch-thick rounds. Cut the rest of the broccoli into bite-size pieces.

Put the broccoli pieces in a small pot, add the water, cover and cook over medium heat for about 4 minutes, or until a sharp knife penetrates a slice of stalk with only a little resistance. Drain in a colander or strainer, run cold water over the broccoli to stop the cooking and drain again. Transfer to a salad bowl.

Cut the avocados lengthwise the whole way around and twist to separate the halves. Discard the pits. Peel the halves and cut them into ½-inch pieces. Add them to the salad bowl.

Peel the onion, cut it lengthwise in half and then cut into thin half-moon slices. Add them to the bowl.

Wash the tomatoes, cut them into eighths and add them to the bowl.

Sprinkle on the salt and pepper, drizzle on some dressing and toss. Serve immediately, or refrigerate until needed.

MOM WARNING

▼

Tomatoes should not be refrigerated because the
cold temperature deadens their flavor. Store them
in a bowl on a counter or shelf, away from
the direct sun, until needed.

Southwestern Coleslaw

SERVES: 4-6

Serve with: Southern Barbecued Pork (page 210)

Preparation Time: 20 minutes (using a food processor) or 30 minutes (by hand) ▼ Cooking Time: 1 minute

Rating: Easy (with a food processor); Not So Easy (by hand) ▼ Can Prepare the Day Before: Yes

I WAS INTRODUCED TO THIS SPICY COLESLAW while helping my sister Bonnie move into her new Phoenix home. After lugging her 1,000-pound fridge across town through 120-degree heat, I collapsed in front of a bowl of this concoction she had created. Nothing had ever tasted so good. She called it Mexican coleslaw, but to avoid being sued by her, I changed the name. I've since served it to guests in my cool apartment, and they appreciate it just as much as I did. You can make it without building up a sweat if you have a food processor.

COLESLAW

1 small (about 1 pound) or ½ large green or red cabbage
 (see Mom Tip 1, page 73) or 16-ounce package shredded cabbage

2 medium carrots

½ medium red onion (see Mom Tip 1)

1 red bell pepper

½ bunch fresh cilantro (see Mom Warning)

1 15-ounce can whole-kernel corn (not creamed corn)

1 4-ounce can diced green chiles

DRESSING

2 tablespoons sugar

2 tablespoons corn oil or olive oil

2   tablespoons balsamic vinegar (see Mom Tip 2)
1   tablespoon prepared mustard
½   teaspoon salt

COLESLAW: Remove and discard the 2 outermost cabbage leaves if they look discolored or damaged. If not, just rinse the cabbage. If you are using a whole cabbage, cut it in half. Remove and discard the solid center core.

Peel the carrots and onion. Wash the red bell pepper, cut it in half and remove and discard the stem and seeds. Wash the cilantro and pat dry between paper towels. Trim and discard the bottom 2 inches of stem.

With a food processor: Use the regular blade, not the shredding one. Cut the cabbage, carrots, onion and red bell pepper into 2-inch chunks. Put one-fourth of these vegetables into the appliance bowl and process for about 10 seconds, or until the vegetables have been cut into ⅛-inch pieces—no longer, or they will turn to mush. Transfer to a large bowl. Repeat the process three more times. During the last chopping session, add the cilantro with the vegetables.

By hand: Use a grater to shred the cabbage, carrots and red bell pepper. Cut the onion and cilantro into ⅛-inch pieces by hand. Transfer the vegetables and cilantro to a large bowl.

Drain and discard the liquid from the corn and green chiles. Add the corn and chiles to the bowl and mix.

DRESSING: Combine the sugar, oil, vinegar, mustard and salt in a small pot and bring to a boil over high heat. Turn off the heat and let cool. Pour the dressing over the vegetables. Mix thoroughly and serve, or refrigerate, covered, until needed.

MOM TIP 1

▼

Red onions are actually purple. They are usually sold individually and can vary in size from a tennis ball to a grapefruit. Their flavor is slightly sweet.

MOM TIP 2

▼

Balsamic vinegar is available at the grocery store. It tastes more mellow than white or cider vinegar. In a pinch, substitute wine vinegar.

MOM WARNING

▼

Don't leave out the fresh cilantro. It's the key to this salad.

Tabouli Salad

SERVES: 4-6

Serve with: Greek Island Fish (page 248) ▼ Preparation Time: 15 minutes

Cooking Time: None ▼ Rating: Easy ▼ Can Prepare the Day Before: Yes

M Y WIFE SAYS that I never like to travel or try new things. Is it my fault that I'm perfectly happy with suburban American life? I get all the international thrills I need at the food court. On one of our safaris to the local galleria, she introduced me to this Middle Eastern salad. Now I make my own version and, like Marco Polo, introduce it to others at my dinner table.

1	cup bulgur wheat (see Mom Tip 1)
1½	cups boiling water
1	cup fresh parsley leaves (see Mom Tip 2)
½	cup fresh mint leaves or 3 tablespoons dried
3	scallions
2	large tomatoes
¼	cup olive oil
¼	cup lemon juice
½	teaspoon salt
¼	teaspoon black pepper

Put the bulgur wheat in a large bowl, add the water and stir. Set aside for 10 minutes while the bulgur absorbs the water. Stir occasionally to help cool the mixture down.

Meanwhile, wash the parsley and mint sprigs, if using fresh mint, and pat them dry between paper towels. Chop the leaves. Wash the scallions. Cut off the root tip and top 2 inches of the green parts and discard them. Cut the remaining white and green parts into ¼-inch pieces. Wash the tomatoes and cut them into ½-inch cubes. Set the herbs and vegetables aside.

Check the bulgur wheat mixture to make sure all the water has been absorbed and it has cooled down to room temperature. If any water remains, stir the mixture and leave for another 10 minutes. If any water remains in the bowl after that, drain the bulgur in a strainer and return it to the bowl.

Add the parsley, mint, scallions and tomatoes to the bulgur. Then add the olive oil, lemon juice, salt and pepper and mix thoroughly. Serve immediately, or refrigerate, covered, until needed.

MOM TIP 1

▼

Bulgur wheat is commonly used in Middle Eastern dishes. It is not always easy to find. Some grocery stores sell it in 1-pound bags in the dried bean or exotic foods section. Delicatessens, ethnic food stores and health food stores often stock it.
It is available in fine and coarse grinds; either works for Tabouli Salad.
Do not buy whole wheat berries.

MOM TIP 2

▼

This measurement doesn't have to be exact. A little more or less parsley won't change the salad very much.

Jody's Potato Salad

SERVES: 4

Serve with: Lamb Souvlakia (page 208) ▼ Preparation Time: 35 minutes

Cooking Time: 25 minutes ▼ Rating: Not So Easy ▼ Can Prepare the Day Before: Yes

My WIFE JODY FEELS that any other recipe is a waste of potatoes. I'm not quite so rigid, but I am a big fan of this salad, a mainstay in her family for three generations. At no time do I feel more a part of her family than when we're all leaning back in our chairs at the kitchen table with potato remnants on our chins. Now, instead of making my mom's potato salad for friends, I make Jody's. There are never any leftovers, much to her chagrin.

2	pounds potatoes (see Mom Tip 1)
2	large eggs
½	cup frozen petite peas
1	medium celery stalk
1	scallion
½	medium cucumber
½	cup mayonnaise
1	teaspoon celery seeds
½	teaspoon salt

Peel the potatoes and cut them in half. Put them in a large pot, cover with water and bring to a boil over high heat. Turn down the heat to medium, cover and cook for 20 to 25 minutes, or until a sharp knife pushed into a potato meets with no resistance. Check the potatoes occasionally and add more water if there's less than an inch left. Drain and then cover them with cold water. When the potatoes are cool enough to handle, drain again. Cut them into ½-inch cubes and put them in a large serving bowl.

Meanwhile, hard-cook the eggs (see Mom Tip 2). Gently place them in a medium pot, cover with water and bring the water to a boil over high heat. Turn down the heat to medium, cover and cook for 3 minutes. Turn off the heat and let the eggs sit in the hot water, covered, for 15 minutes.

Drain the eggs and cover them with cold water. When they are cool to the touch, peel and cut them into ½-inch pieces. Add them to the serving bowl.

While the potatoes and eggs are cooking, cook the frozen peas according to the package directions (about 5 minutes) and drain them. After they have cooled, add them to the bowl.

Wash the celery. Trim off and discard the ends, cut the stalk into ¼-inch slices and add to the bowl.

Wash the scallion. Cut off the root tip and top 2 inches of the green part and discard them. Cut the remaining white and green parts into ¼-inch pieces and add them to the bowl.

Peel the cucumber and slice lengthwise in half. Scrape out and discard the seeds. Cut the cucumber into ½-inch cubes and add them to the bowl.

Add the mayonnaise, celery seeds and salt and mix thoroughly. Serve immediately, or refrigerate, covered, until needed.

MOM TIP 1

▼

Potatoes are sold in 5- and 10-pound bags, as well as loose. In most cases, the bags are considerably cheaper than the equivalent amount of loose potatoes. For potato salad, I prefer White Rose, Yukon Gold or red potatoes because they hold their shape better than russet potatoes. But all potatoes are good in potato salad.

MOM TIP 2

▼

If I'm boiling potatoes and hard-cooking eggs at the same time, I sometimes combine them. This is what I do: when I put the potatoes on to boil, I add the eggs as well. Once the water comes to a boil, I let the eggs boil for 10 minutes, then fish them out with a large spoon and immerse them in a bowl of cold water to stop the cooking. (The potatoes continue to cook for at least another 10 minutes.) When eggs are cooked this way, sometimes they're jostled around in the water and they crack so that bits of egg white ooze out of the shell. However, they're still perfectly edible.

Salade Niçoise

SERVES: 4 AS A MAIN COURSE

Serve with: Spinach Quiche (page 268) ▼ Preparation Time: 15 minutes

Cooking Time: 25 minutes ▼ Rating: Not So Easy ▼ Can Prepare the Day Before: No

A YEAR AGO, my parents took in a French exchange student. He and a hundred other French kids had been flown to Los Angeles and left at the airport. No one had bothered to arrange families for them to stay with. So my parents took pity on a teenager named Thibault. His English was limited. He knew "Hello," "Thank you" and "Baywatch." By the time he left, he was able to say, "You make me puke" and "Hey, baby, you rock my world." He taught me to say, *"Je suis un imbécile Américain."* French is such a beautiful language. My mom made Salade Niçoise for Thibault. He'd never had it before.

½	pound fresh green beans
1	pound (3-4 medium) potatoes (see Mom Tip 1)
¼	medium red onion
3	medium tomatoes
2	hard-cooked eggs; see page 105 for directions on how to hard-cook eggs (optional)
4	anchovy fillets (see Mom Tip 2)
½	head leaf lettuce
1	6¼-ounce can tuna
12	black olives (see Mom Tip 2, page 95)
	Easy Italian Dressing (page 109)
	Dash salt
	Dash black pepper

Fill a large pot half-full of water, cover and begin heating over high heat. You can speed up the process by using hot water to start with.

While you're waiting for the water to come to a boil (5 to 10 minutes), wash the beans. Snap ¼ inch off each end and pull; if a string comes off, throw it away with the ends.

Add the beans to the boiling water and boil, uncovered, for about 5 minutes, or until they have softened slightly but still have some crunch. Using a slotted spoon, lift the beans from the boiling water into a strainer, leaving the boiling water in the pot. Run cold water over the beans to stop the cooking. Drain and set aside.

Add the unpeeled potatoes to the boiling water, cover and cook for about 20 minutes, or until a sharp knife pushed into a potato meets with no resistance. Check the potatoes occasionally and add more water if there's less than an inch left. Drain and then cover with cold water. When they are cool enough to handle, drain again and pull the skin off with your fingers or peel it off with a small knife. Cut the potatoes into ½-inch cubes and set aside.

Cut the beans in half. Peel and thinly slice the onion and cut the slices into 1-inch pieces. Wash the tomatoes and cut them into quarters. Cut the hard-cooked eggs into thin slices. Cut the anchovies into ¼-inch pieces and put in a small dish. Set aside.

Separate the lettuce leaves, wash them and pat them dry with paper towels. Cut into bite-size pieces and put them in a large salad bowl. Add the tuna, eggs, olives, onion, tomatoes and beans, then place the potatoes on top.

Pour on ¼ cup salad dressing and toss thoroughly. If the salad seems too dry, add more dressing. Season with salt and pepper and serve immediately, or refrigerate, covered, until needed. Serve the anchovies separately with the salad.

Mom Tip 1

▼

The best potatoes to use for
Salade Niçoise are White Rose or
red potatoes because they hold their
shape. Russet potatoes can get mushy,
especially if they're overcooked.
You could also use baby red or white
potatoes, which are about 1 inch
in diameter. If you scrub baby potatoes
well before cooking, you don't need to
peel them before putting them
in the salad. However, do cut
them in half after they are cooked
(about 10 minutes).

Mom Tip 2

▼

Getting a whole room of people
together who all like anchovies is
impossible, so I usually serve them
on a separate dish and let people
decide for themselves. The salad
tastes good with or without them.

Easy Italian Dressing

MAKES: ½ CUP

Preparation Time: 5 minutes ▼ Cooking Time: None
Rating: Very Easy ▼ Can Prepare the Day Before: Yes

EASY MEANS EASY. I always keep oil and vinegar around, so it takes two seconds to whip this up. It sounds more impressive if you call it "vinaigrette."

2   tablespoons red wine vinegar (see Mom Tip)
½   teaspoon salt
¼   teaspoon black pepper
½   cup olive oil

Combine the vinegar, salt and pepper in a small bowl and beat them with a fork. Slowly add the oil, beating continuously, until it is incorporated. Keep any extra dressing in a closed container in the refrigerator and shake or beat with a fork before using.

MOM TIP

▼

Here are some ways to vary Easy Italian Dressing:

▼ Substitute 2 tablespoons lemon juice for the wine vinegar for a lighter, lemony flavor.

▼ Add 2 teaspoons chopped fresh dill, basil or mint after you have mixed in the oil.

▼ Add ¼ teaspoon dry mustard with the salt and pepper.

▼ Add 1 small garlic clove, finely chopped, with the salt and pepper.

▼ Add 3 tablespoons whipping (not whipped) cream after you have mixed in the oil.

Simple French Dressing

MAKES: 3-3½ CUPS

Preparation Time: 10 minutes ▼ Cooking Time: None

Rating: Very Easy ▼ Can Prepare the Day Before: Yes

YOU'VE HEARD OF HAVING SOUP AND SALAD as a light lunch. Well, how about soup *in* your salad? This recipe, from my mom's friend Carol Mead, has a canned-soup base, but no one would guess it.

1	small onion
1	10-ounce can condensed tomato soup
1	cup corn oil or vegetable oil
¾	cup sugar
½	cup white vinegar
1	tablespoon dry mustard
1	tablespoon Worcestershire sauce
1	teaspoon salt

Peel and thinly slice the onion. Put it in the appliance bowl of a blender or food processor. Add the tomato soup, oil, sugar, vinegar, mustard, Worcestershire sauce and salt and process until well blended, about 15 seconds. Keep any extra dressing in a closed container in the refrigerator and shake or beat with a fork before using.

Thousand Island Dressing

MAKES: ½ CUP

Preparation Time: 5 minutes ▼ Cooking Time: None
Rating: Very Easy ▼ Can Prepare the Day Before: Yes

THIS DRESSING MAY BE THE SIMPLEST EVER, but why make things complicated? I order Thousand Island when I go to restaurants, so why not make it at home? It's not the most sophisticated salad dressing, but everybody likes it.

¼   cup mayonnaise
¼   cup ketchup
2   tablespoons sweet relish

Combine the mayonnaise, ketchup and relish in a small bowl and mix thoroughly with a fork so that no blobs of mayonnaise show. Keep extra dressing in a closed container in the refrigerator.

Potatoes / Rice / Bread

P OTATOES, RICE AND BREAD DO THE HEAVY LIFTING in a meal. The entrées and cute little appetizers get all the credit, but the starch dishes provide the real substance. They're the Rosencrantz and Guildenstern of dinner. Sometimes, though, they can take on a larger role. If your main course isn't as good as you'd planned, use that old magician's trick: misdirection. Just keep offering the side dish: "Pay no attention to the overcooked shrimp. Have some more Caribbean Rice!" Pretty soon, your guests will forget which dish was the entrée.

Recipes

Fried Potatoes and Onions

SERVES: 4

Serve with: Old-Fashioned Brisket with Barbecue Sauce (page 200)

Preparation Time: 10 minutes ▼ Cooking Time: 10 minutes

Rating: Very Easy ▼ Can Prepare the Day Before: No

MY MOM INVENTED THIS RECIPE when she had guests coming over and she'd forgotten to bake the potatoes. I don't think I'd be able to concoct something original with company breathing down my neck. I'd probably shrug and serve the potatoes raw, calling them "Potatoes Tartare." This dish is a great alternative to baked potatoes, and it's a lot faster.

4   medium potatoes (see Mom Tip)

1   large onion

¼   cup olive oil or corn oil

   Dash salt

Peel the potatoes and cut them into ½-inch-thick slices. Cut each slice into ½-inch-wide strips and each strip into ½-inch pieces. Peel the onion and slice into ¼-inch-thick slices. Cut each slice into ½-inch pieces.

Pour the oil into a large frying pan and heat over medium-high heat. After 1 minute, carefully put 1 potato cube into the pan. If it immediately begins to sizzle, add the rest of the potatoes and the onions. If it doesn't sizzle, wait another 30 seconds and try a second cube. (If the oil isn't hot enough, the potatoes will stick to the bottom of the pan.) When the oil is hot enough, add the potatoes and onions and cook for about 1 minute, or until those on the bottom start to brown. Turn them over with a spatula and continue cooking, turning them every minute or so, for about 6 minutes, or until they are golden brown. They will cook quickly, because the pieces are small. If they start to burn, turn down the heat to medium.

Drain the potato-onion mixture on paper towels, sprinkle with salt and serve immediately.

Mom Tip

▼

Leftover baked or boiled potatoes
can be used instead of raw potatoes.
The cooking time is about the same.

Garlic Mashed Potatoes

SERVES: 4

Serve with: Hungarian Goulash (page 194)   ▼   Preparation Time: 20 minutes

Cooking Time: 20 minutes   ▼   Rating: Very Easy   ▼   Can Prepare the Day Before: No

WHEN MY SISTER BONNIE and her husband Tom visited us in St. Louis, Jody and I wanted to show off our temporary hometown. We took them to the Gateway Arch and the Bowling Hall of Fame. But their strongest memory will always be the restaurant we ate at, a place called Saleem's, whose slogan is "Where Garlic is King." Tom ignored Bonnie's no-kiss warnings and devoured a whole head of baked garlic. It left a strong impression on both him and Bonnie.

This dish is a good middle ground between boring mashed potatoes and crazy garlic obsession.

4	large or 8 medium potatoes
4	garlic cloves (see Mom Tip 1)
½	cup milk + more if needed
¼	cup (½ stick) butter or margarine
½	teaspoon salt
¼	teaspoon black pepper

Peel the potatoes and cut them into 2-inch chunks. Put the chunks into a large pot and cover with water. Bring to a boil over high heat. Turn down the heat to medium, cover and cook for about 20 minutes, or until a sharp knife pushed into a potato meets with no resistance. Check the potatoes occasionally and add more water if there's less than an inch left. When the potatoes are cooked, drain them and leave them in the pot, covered, to stay hot. Meanwhile, peel and finely chop the garlic.

Heat the milk, butter or margarine, garlic, salt and pepper in a small pot over medium heat until the butter or margarine melts. Remove from the heat and set aside.

Mash the potatoes with a masher or a fork, trying to get out most of the lumps. Add the milk mixture and beat until creamy. If the potatoes seem too thick and heavy, add a few more tablespoons milk (see Mom Tip 2). Serve immediately.

MOM TIP 1

▼

I've recently discovered bottled crushed garlic. For years, I insisted on using fresh garlic cloves. Now I happily spoon out already peeled and mashed fresh garlic. A great time-saver, it's available in bottles in the vegetable or gourmet department. Keep it in the refrigerator after it's opened. One-half teaspoon crushed garlic equals 1 garlic clove.

MOM TIP 2

▼

Here are a few other possible ways to glamorize your mashed potatoes:

▼ Mix 1 cup grated cheddar or Monterey Jack cheese into the hot potatoes.

▼ Mix ¼ cup bottled horseradish into the hot potatoes.

▼ Use cream instead of milk when mashing the potatoes.

Potatoes au Gratin

SERVES: 4

Serve with: Beef Bourguignon (page 192) ▼ Preparation Time: 15 minutes

Cooking Time: 50-60 minutes ▼ Rating: Easy ▼ Can Prepare the Day Before: Yes

IN COLLEGE, my roommates all had different styles of cooking. Mike and Paul would spend hours planning menus and preparing things with more than two ingredients. I would peel off the top of a cup of ramen soup and add hot water. Scott would toast his Pop-Tarts. And Adam would open a box of potatoes au gratin. We all thought he was a snob for eating French food.

Despite his lawyer's salary, Adam still eats like an astronaut. This recipe may come as a shock to him, but you can make Potatoes au Gratin from real potatoes instead of adding water to freeze-dried potato flakes. Our recipe has no chemical compounds. It's just potatoes, onions, milk and cheese. But through the magic of real cooking, this mixture turns into an impressive side dish.

4	medium potatoes
1	medium onion
1	tablespoon corn oil or vegetable oil
½	teaspoon salt
¼	teaspoon black pepper
1	cup grated Swiss or cheddar cheese (4 ounces)
½	cup milk

Preheat the oven to 375 degrees.

Peel the potatoes and cut into ¼-inch-thick slices. Peel the onion and cut into ¼-inch-thick slices.

Spread the oil over the bottom and sides of a 9-inch pie pan or 1-quart casserole dish (see Mom Tip). Arrange half the potato slices in the bottom of the pan, overlapping them slightly. Arrange half the onion slices on top of the potato slices. Sprinkle with salt and pepper and then cover with half of the grated cheese. Arrange the remaining potato slices on top of the cheese, then add the remaining onion slices. Sprinkle with salt and pepper and cover with the rest of the grated cheese. Pour the milk on top.

Bake, uncovered, for 50 to 60 minutes. The potatoes are done when they can easily be pierced with a fork and the top layer is brown and crispy. Serve immediately, or keep warm in a 200-degree oven until needed.

MOM TIP

▼

If a casserole isn't marked "1 quart" or "2 quarts,"
you can tell how big it is by adding water, cup by cup,
until it is full. A 1-quart casserole holds 4 cups of water;
a 2-quart casserole holds 8 cups of water.

Spicy Potatoes

SERVES: 4

Serve with: Barbecued Chicken (page 218) ▼ Preparation Time: 15 minutes

Cooking Time: 25 minutes ▼ Rating: Easy ▼ Can Prepare the Day Before: Yes

SOMETIMES IT'S GOOD TO LET THE POTATOES BE THE STAR. Spicy Potatoes attract attention, and they deserve it.

1	small onion
1	garlic clove
½	red or green bell pepper
2	tablespoons corn oil or vegetable oil
1	teaspoon chili powder
1	teaspoon ground coriander
1	teaspoon cumin seeds
1	teaspoon mustard seeds
½	teaspoon ground ginger
¼	teaspoon ground turmeric
1	8-ounce can tomato sauce
1	pound small (1½ inches in diameter) potatoes (see Mom Tip)
	Up to ¼ cup water (optional)

Peel the onion and cut it into ¼-inch pieces. Peel and finely chop the garlic. Wash the bell pepper and cut into ¼-inch pieces.

Heat the oil in a large frying pan over medium heat. Add the onion, garlic and bell pepper and cook for about 5 minutes, stirring occasionally, until the vegetables begin to soften.

Add the chili powder, coriander, cumin seeds, mustard seeds, ginger and turmeric and stir until they have been absorbed. Add the tomato sauce and stir.

While the sauce is heating, wash the potatoes thoroughly but do not peel them.

Add the potatoes to the sauce, stir and bring to a boil. Turn down the heat to medium-low, cover and cook for about 20 minutes, or until the largest potato can easily be pierced with a fork. Check the potatoes after 10 minutes; if the sauce seems to be boiling away, add some water. Serve immediately, or let cool and reheat when needed.

Mom Tip

▼

If you can't find small potatoes, which are often
called new potatoes, substitute regular red or white
potatoes (not russet potatoes), cut into quarters.

Lemon Rice

SERVES: 4

Serve with: Tandoori Chicken (page 231) ▼ Preparation Time: 5 minutes

Cooking Time: 20 minutes ▼ Rating: Very Easy

Can Prepare the Day Before: Yes (see Mom Warning)

LEMON RICE IS THE ONLY FLUORESCENT RECIPE in the book. It's the turmeric, not the lemon juice, that makes this rice brighter than the sun. It tastes like you'd imagine it would: a little bit lemony and a little bit rice.

1¾	cups water
1	cup long-grain rice (see Mom Tip 1, page 127)
¼	cup lemon juice
½	teaspoon salt
¼	teaspoon ground turmeric
2	tablespoons olive oil or corn oil
½	cup cashew nuts
½	teaspoon mustard seeds

Put the water in a medium pot, cover and bring to a boil. Add the rice, lemon juice, salt and turmeric and return the water to a boil, then stir, cover and turn down the heat to low. Cook for 15 minutes. Remove from the heat and let the rice sit, covered, for another 5 minutes to finish cooking.

Meanwhile, heat the oil in a small frying pan or pot over medium-high heat. Add the cashews and mustard seeds. Cook for about 2 minutes, stirring frequently, until the nuts begin to turn light brown. If the mustard seeds start popping out of the pan, put on a lid. Add the nut mixture to the rice, stir and serve.

Mom Warning

▼

If you are cooking Lemon Rice more than an hour
ahead of time, don't add the cashew mixture until
just before serving. Cashews get soggy
if they sit in rice.

Caribbean Rice

SERVES: 4

Serve with: Sweet-and-Sour Country-Style Pork Ribs (page 212) ▼ Preparation Time: 25 minutes

Cooking Time: 25 minutes ▼ Rating: Easy ▼ Can Prepare the Day Before: Yes

WHAT MAKES THIS SUBSTANTIAL RICE CARIBBEAN? The black beans, the bananas and the spices. It may seem strange to put bananas in a nondessert dish, but when cooked, they blend into the rice and are delicious.

¼ cup canned black beans (see Mom Tip)

1 small onion

1 medium carrot

1 medium celery stalk

2 garlic cloves

3 tablespoons olive oil

1 cup long-grain rice (see Mom Tip 1, page 126)

½ teaspoon salt

¼ teaspoon black pepper

¼ teaspoon ground cinnamon

¼ teaspoon ground cumin

¼ teaspoon dried oregano

¼ teaspoon dried thyme

⅛ teaspoon red pepper flakes

2 cups water

2 bananas

2   scallions

¼   cup chopped fresh cilantro

Drain the beans and rinse them in a strainer or colander under cold running water and set aside.

Peel the onion and carrot and cut them into ¼-inch pieces. Wash the celery stalk, trim off and discard the ends and cut it into ¼-inch slices. Peel and finely chop the garlic.

Heat 2 tablespoons of the oil in a medium pot over medium heat. Add the onion, carrot, celery and garlic and cook for about 5 minutes, stirring occasionally, until the vegetables begin to soften.

Add the rice and stir for about 1 minute until it is coated with oil. Add the salt, pepper, cinnamon, cumin, oregano, thyme and red pepper flakes and stir until they have been absorbed. Add the beans and water and bring the mixture to a boil over high heat. Turn down the heat to low, cover and cook for 15 minutes (see Mom Warning). Remove from the heat and let the rice sit, covered, for another 5 minutes to finish cooking.

While the rice is cooking, peel the bananas and cut them into ½-inch-thick slices. Wash the scallions. Cut off the root tips and the top 2 inches of the green parts and discard them. Cut the remaining white and green parts into ¼-inch pieces. Set aside.

Heat the remaining 1 tablespoon oil in a small frying pan over medium heat. Add the bananas and cook for about 1 minute per side, or until they begin to brown. Remove from the heat.

Check the rice to make sure it is done and all the liquid has been absorbed. If not, cook for another 2 minutes over medium heat. Stir in the bananas, scallions and cilantro with a fork, and serve.

MOM TIP

▼

To make Caribbean Rice into
a vegetarian main dish instead
of a side dish, add the full
15-ounce can of beans.

MOM WARNING

▼

Don't stir the rice in the
middle of cooking or it will
become sticky.

Pacific Rim Rice Pilaf

SERVES: 4

Serve with: Barbecued Chicken (page 218) ▼ **Preparation Time:** 10 minutes

Cooking Time: 25 minutes ▼ **Rating:** Easy ▼ **Can Prepare the Day Before:** Yes

SOME PEOPLE GET A KICK out of using chopsticks. I've never been able to figure them out, so I rarely try. But when I serve Chinese food, I like to offer guests the option. After all, I've saved enough free chopsticks from bags of takeout to cater a Chinese wedding.

Because the pilaf doesn't stick together, however, your guests may have to painstakingly try to latch onto one grain at a time—although the raisins and onions offer bigger targets. All in all, it's probably best to provide forks. But this dish tastes good enough to eat with your fingers.

- 1 small onion *½ C minced onion*
- 2 garlic cloves
- 3 scallions
- 2 tablespoons butter or margarine
- 1 cup long-grain rice (see Mom Tip 1)
- ¼ cup raisins
- 2 cups water
- 2 tablespoons soy sauce
- 1 teaspoon sesame oil (see Mom Tip 1, page 143)
- ½ teaspoon chili powder

Peel and finely slice the onion. Peel and finely chop the garlic. Wash the scallions. Cut off the root tips and the top 2 inches of the green parts and discard them. Cut the remaining white and green parts into ¼-inch pieces. Set the scallions aside.

Heat the butter or margarine in a medium pot over medium heat. Add the onion and garlic and cook for about 5 minutes, stirring occasionally, until they begin to soften.

Add the rice and stir for about 1 minute, until it is coated with butter or margarine (see Mom Tip 2). Add the raisins, water, soy sauce, sesame oil and chili powder, stir and bring to a boil over high heat. Turn down the heat to low, cover and cook, without stirring, for 15 minutes (see Mom Warning). Remove from the heat and let the rice sit, covered, for another 5 minutes to finish cooking.

Check the rice to make sure it is done and all the liquid has been absorbed. If not, cook for another 2 minutes over medium heat. Stir in the scallions with a fork, and serve.

MOM TIP 1
▼

Long-grain rice is available plain or in exotic varieties such as basmati, which has a distinctive nutty flavor, and jasmine, which has a perfumed flavor.

MOM TIP 2
▼

Coating rice in butter, margarine or oil before adding water cooks the starch at the surface of the grains and thereby helps keep them fluffy and separate, which is what makes pilaf pilaf.

MOM WARNING
▼

Don't stir the rice in the middle of cooking or it will become sticky.

Lebanese Spiced Rice

SERVES: 4

Serve with: Lamb Souvlakia (page 208) ▼ Preparation Time: 20 minutes

Cooking Time: 25 minutes ▼ Rating: Easy ▼ Can Prepare the Day Before: Yes

THIS DISH COMES FROM OUR FRIENDS the Prochniks. I grew up with their son Simon. While I was seeing how many Legos I could arrange in a column, he was building Lego renderings of the Hanging Gardens of Babylon. Sometimes when my parents came to pick me up, the Prochniks would invite us to stay for dinner. His mother would make elaborate dishes like Lebanese Spiced Rice, while my mom served only plain.

My mom has since caught up, and I have too.

1	teaspoon cardamom seeds (see Mom Tip 1)
1	teaspoon whole black peppercorns
1	teaspoon whole cloves
2	tablespoons olive oil
1	cup long-grain rice (see Mom Tip 1, page 127)
1½	cups water
6	fresh cilantro sprigs
2	tablespoons sweetened shredded coconut (see Mom Tip 2)
2	tablespoons cashew nuts
2	tablespoons lemon juice

If the cardamom seeds are still in their pods, crack open the pods and remove the seeds. Discard the pods. Put the cardamom seeds, peppercorns and cloves in a small dry frying pan and heat over high heat for about 3 minutes, or until they start to jump around in the pan. Remove from the heat (see Mom Tip 3).

If you have a spice grinder, an unused pepper mill or a mortar and pestle, grind the spices that way. Otherwise, when the spices have cooled, put them in a small heavy self-sealing plastic storage bag or wrap them in several layers of plastic wrap, making sure they're well enclosed. Then hit the spices with a hammer, a rolling pin or some other heavy object to smash them into tiny pieces.

Heat the oil in a medium pot over medium heat. Add the spices and rice and stir for about 1 minute, until the rice is coated with oil. Add the water (see Mom Tip 4) and bring to a boil over high heat. Turn down the heat to low, cover and cook for 15 minutes. Remove from the heat and let the rice sit, covered, for 5 minutes to finish cooking.

While the rice is cooking, wash the cilantro sprigs and pat them dry between paper towels. Cut off and discard the stems and cut the leafy parts into ½-inch pieces.

Check the rice to make sure it is done and all the liquid has been absorbed. If not, cook for another 2 minutes over medium heat. Stir in the cilantro, coconut, cashews and lemon juice with a fork, and serve.

MOM TIP 1

▼

Cardamom seeds are available at Indian delicatessens, gourmet food shops and in some supermarket spice racks. A bottle is very expensive, but you may be able to find a small packet for a few dollars. The seeds are usually left in their pods, which are either green or white. You need 6 or 7 pods to make 1 teaspoon of seeds, or you could use ¼ teaspoon ground cardamom.

MOM TIP 2

▼

Shredded coconut is available in plastic bags on a shelf near the chocolate chips.

MOM TIP 3

▼

Heating the spices before grinding them brings out their flavor.

MOM TIP 4

▼

If you boil water separately in a kettle and add it hot to the rice mixture, it will return to the boil within moments.

Middle Eastern Bulgur Wheat Pilaf

SERVES: 4

Serve with: Chicken Satay with Peanut Sauce (page 220)

Preparation Time: 15 minutes ▼ Cooking Time: 12 minutes

Rating: Very Easy ▼ Can Prepare the Day Before: Yes

I FIRST ATE THIS DISH SURROUNDED BY NUDES. No, I wasn't in a Middle Eastern strip club. I was visiting a childhood friend in London. His mother—who used to be just another mom pushing her kid on the swing—had become a successful artist, and her apartment was full of stylish paintings of naked women.

The food she served was equally exotic. What made the strongest impression was this Middle Eastern dish of bulgur. As an artist, she could never settle for plain rice. When I serve this for my own guests, I point out the painting she gave Jody and me for a wedding gift. She gave us a choice, and we picked the one with the most clothes.

1	small carrot
1	scallion
1	tablespoon olive oil
1	cup bulgur wheat (see Mom Tip 1, page 103)
1½	cups water
½	teaspoon salt
	Dash black pepper

Peel the carrot and grate it on the largest holes of the grater. Wash the scallion. Cut off the root tip and the top 2 inches of the green parts and discard them. Cut the remaining parts into ¼-inch pieces.

Heat the oil in a medium pot over medium-high heat. Add the carrot and scallion and cook for 2 minutes, until the vegetables just begin to soften.

Add the bulgur wheat and stir so that it absorbs any excess oil. Then add the water, salt and pepper. Turn down the heat to medium-low, cover and cook for about 10 minutes, or until all the water has been absorbed. If any water is left at the end of 10 minutes, remove the lid and cook for another 1 to 2 minutes, stirring occasionally, until it evaporates. Serve immediately, or let cool and reheat over low heat when needed.

Mom Tip

▼

Instead of carrots and scallions, you can use a
small onion or ½ red or green bell pepper.

Corn Bread

SERVES: 8

Serve with: Mexican Grilled Cornish Hens (page 224)

Preparation Time: 10 minutes ▼ Cooking Time: 20 minutes

Rating: Very Easy ▼ Can Prepare the Day Before: Yes

ORN BREAD IS THE UNIVERSAL SIDE DISH. It seems to go with everything. It's particularly ideal for serving with meat dishes, because the bread can sop up the gravy. That way, it not only tastes good but also helps you clean up.

1	cup all-purpose flour + 1 teaspoon for dusting pan
1	cup yellow cornmeal (see Mom Tip)
2	teaspoons baking powder
½	teaspoon baking soda
½	teaspoon salt
1	cup milk
1	tablespoon lemon juice
¼	cup honey
1	large egg
3	tablespoons corn oil or vegetable oil + more for greasing pan

Place an oven rack in the middle position and preheat the oven to 425 degrees.

Combine the flour, cornmeal, baking powder, baking soda and salt in a large bowl and set aside.

Pour the milk into a small bowl, add the lemon juice and stir. Add the honey, egg and oil and stir until well combined. Add the liquid mixture to the flour mixture and stir vigorously with a wooden spoon or fork until smooth.

Lightly rub the bottom and sides of a 10-x-6-inch, 9-inch square or 8-inch square pan with oil. Sprinkle with the 1 teaspoon flour and swirl it around, coating the oiled surfaces, to keep the bread from sticking. Pour the batter into the pan and shake the pan from side to side several times to make sure the batter spreads to all corners.

Bake for 20 minutes, or until a cake tester or knife comes out clean when inserted into the center and the top has begun to brown. Remove from the oven, cut into squares and serve immediately, or let cool. Serve with honey or butter. Refrigerate any leftovers.

MOM TIP

▼

Cornmeal comes in yellow and white varieties
and is available in boxes near the flour.

Honey Spice Bread

SERVES: 8-10

Serve with: Omelets (page 260)

Preparation Time: 10 minutes (using a food processor or mixer) or 15 minutes (by hand)

Cooking Time: 50-60 minutes ▼ Rating: Very Easy

Can Prepare the Day Before: Yes

THE IDEA OF MAKING BREAD seems daunting: dealing with the yeast, kneading the dough and waiting for it to rise. But Honey Spice Bread isn't like that. You don't have to mess around with the voodoo of yeast. This is easy to make. Just stir and bake. And one of the hidden benefits of this bread is that it keeps very well in the fridge.

3	cups all-purpose flour + 1 teaspoon for dusting pan
¼	cup dark brown sugar
1	teaspoon baking soda
1	teaspoon ground cinnamon
½	teaspoon ground nutmeg
½	teaspoon ground cloves
¼	teaspoon salt
¾	cup honey
1	5-ounce can evaporated milk (see Mom Tip)
⅓	cup milk
	Oil for greasing pan

Place an oven rack in the middle position and preheat the oven to 350 degrees.

With a food processor or electric mixer: Put the flour, brown sugar, baking soda, cinnamon, nutmeg, cloves and salt in the appliance bowl. Add the honey, evaporated milk and milk and process or mix until thoroughly combined.

By hand: Put the flour, brown sugar, baking soda, cinnamon, nutmeg, cloves and salt in a large bowl. Add the honey, evaporated milk and milk and mix thoroughly with a large wooden or other heavy spoon.

Lightly rub the bottom and sides of an 8¼-inch-x-4½-inch or similar-size bread pan with oil. Sprinkle with the 1 teaspoon flour and swirl it around, coating the oiled surfaces, to keep the bread from sticking.

Bake for about 50 minutes, or until the sides of the bread begin pulling away from the pan and a cake tester or a knife inserted into the middle of the bread comes out clean. (If you have used a slightly smaller pan, the bread may need to bake for an extra 5 to 10 minutes.) Remove from the oven.

Run a knife around the sides of the bread, loosening it from the pan, and tip the bread onto a wire rack and turn right side up. When the bread has cooled to room temperature, wrap it in plastic wrap and store in the refrigerator until needed. Thinly slice and serve plain or with butter or cream cheese. Tightly wrapped and refrigerated, this bread keeps for months.

MOM TIP

▼

Evaporated milk looks like a cross between thick cream
and syrup, but it is actually unsweetened milk with a reduced
water content. It provides richness without excessive calories.
It's found in the canned-milk section, often near the
baking supplies, and is useful to keep around
in case you run out of regular milk.

Vegetables

VEGETABLES ARE A PART OF MOST PEOPLE'S DIET—there's just no way around that. So despite my childish aversion to most green foods, when I'm cooking for others, I have to provide some nutrition along the way. And, alas, as I move into higher age brackets, I, too, am beginning to realize that there are just not enough vitamins in pizza sauce to keep me healthy. When I compete in 10K races, I'm no longer matched with 18-year-olds. I'm now in the same category as 35-year-olds. How did I age 17 years overnight? To reverse the effects of aging, I recently ate a whole plate of asparagus.

Perhaps in a reaction to her own childhood, when most of the vegetables she ate came out of a can, my mom has scoured the earth looking for vegetable dishes like Gujerati Beans and Spicy Asian Baby Bok Choy. Hopefully, you won't have to rap any of your guests' knuckles to get them to chow down.

▲
Recipes
▼

Cranberry Sauce

SERVES: 6-8

Serve with: Mexican Grilled Cornish Hens (page 224) ▼ Preparation Time: 5 minutes
Cooking Time: 10 minutes ▼ Rating: Very Easy ▼ Can Prepare the Day Before: Yes

CRANBERRY SAUCE is a traditional Thanksgiving and Christmas side dish, but there's no law that it can be served only on holidays. That's like saying you can eat ice cream only for dessert. One of the good things about being an adult is you can write the menu. Your guests might be surprised to see cranberry sauce next to Grilled Salmon or Chicken Kiev, but they'll forget tradition once they taste it.

Many people seem happy with store-bought cranberry sauce. I always find it disturbing to eat food that comes in the shape of a can. And this is so easy to make, you can take that can out of your cupboard and donate it to a food drive.

1   12-ounce package fresh cranberries (see Mom Tip)
1   cup sugar
1   cup water (see Mom Warning)

Rinse the cranberries in cold water. Drain, put them in a medium pot and pick through them, removing and discarding any stems and shriveled or moldy berries. Add the sugar and water and stir thoroughly to dissolve the sugar.

Heat over medium-high heat, stirring occasionally, until the berries begin to pop. The first berry should pop in 4 to 5 minutes. The rest will pop within the next 5 minutes. When most of the berries have popped, you can speed up the final popping by pressing the remaining whole berries against the side of the pot with a large spoon. Watch out for spattering juice.

When all the berries have popped, remove the pot from the heat and let cool. Stir thoroughly and refrigerate. Transfer to a serving bowl and serve cold.

MOM TIP

▼

Bags of fresh cranberries are
usually available in the vegetable
department from October to January.
They freeze well, so if you're a
cranberry sauce addict, buy some
extra bags and toss them into
the freezer for use in the summer.
Cook them straight
from the freezer.

MOM WARNING

▼

Kevin's grandmother always
had problems with making
cranberry sauce because she
would add too much water.
The resulting mixture was more
like cranberry juice than sauce.
These measurements
are important.

Simple Snow Peas

SERVES: 4

Serve with: Chicken with Red Wine (page 228) ▼ Preparation Time: 10 minutes

Cooking Time: 2 minutes ▼ Rating: Very Easy ▼ Can Prepare the Day Before: No

MY MOM THOUGHT I SHOULD EXPLAIN what snow peas are. I told her that anyone with the motor skills to get to the supermarket would already know what they were. But in case you slipped through the cracks, they're flat green pea pods about three inches long, with minuscule peas inside. And they're just about the easiest vegetable to prepare.

½ pound fresh snow peas (see Mom Tip)
1 tablespoon butter or margarine
Dash salt
Dash black pepper

Half-fill a medium pot with hot water, cover and begin heating over high heat.

Rinse the snow peas. Pull the strings off each side by snapping the top ¼ inch from each end and pulling firmly down each edge.

When the water is boiling, add the snow peas. Cook for 2 minutes, then immediately drain. Cooked snow peas should be crunchy, not mushy. Add the butter or margarine, salt and pepper, stir and serve.

MOM TIP

▼

The smaller the pea pods, the more tender they are.

Snow peas are often sold loose, so you can pick out the ones you want.

Choose similar-size pods so they will cook at the same rate.

Fried Cherry Tomatoes

SERVES: 4

Serve with: Crunchy Baked Fish (page 252) ▼ Preparation Time: 10 minutes

Cooking Time: 3 minutes ▼ Rating: Very Easy ▼ Can Prepare the Day Before: No

TOMATOES DON'T JUST BELONG IN SALADS. They make a good side dish all by themselves. But to make regular tomatoes bite-size, you have to cut them up, which causes the inside to dribble out. Cherry tomatoes have the advantage of already being bite-size, so your guests can pop them into their mouths like bonbons.

4   scallions
1   12-ounce basket cherry tomatoes
1   tablespoon olive oil
1   teaspoon sugar (see Mom Tip)
½   teaspoon salt
½   teaspoon dried basil

Wash the scallions. Cut off the root tip and the top 2 inches of the green parts and discard them. Cut the remaining white and green parts into ½-inch pieces. Wash and pat the cherry tomatoes dry with paper towels. Remove and discard any stems.

Heat the oil in a large frying pan over medium heat. Add the scallions, tomatoes, sugar, salt and basil and cook for about 3 minutes, shaking the pan occasionally, or until the tomatoes are hot but the skins haven't burst. Serve immediately.

MOM TIP

▼

Sugar brings out the natural sweetness of tomatoes.

Stir-Fried Asparagus

SERVES: 4

Serve with: Asian Turkey Burgers with Ginger Soy Sauce (page 240) ▼ Preparation Time: 10 minutes

Cooking Time: 3 minutes ▼ Rating: Very Easy ▼ Can Prepare the Day Before: Yes

I'M NOT A BIG FAN OF LONG, DROOPY BOILED ASPARAGUS. In this recipe, you cut the spears up, flavor them with Asian spices and turn the asparagus into a much better vegetable. This isn't the chaotic, panic-inducing kind of stir-fry. It's one of the easiest around.

1 pound fresh asparagus

2 garlic cloves

1 tablespoon peanut oil or corn oil

¼ teaspoon red pepper flakes (optional)

1 teaspoon soy sauce

1 teaspoon sesame oil (see Mom Tip 1)

Rinse the asparagus thoroughly, being careful not to break off any of the tips. Trim off and discard any white part from the bottom of each stalk, usually 1 to 2 inches (see Mom Tip 2). Cut each stalk diagonally into 2-inch lengths. Peel and finely chop the garlic. Set aside.

Heat the oil in a wok or large frying pan over high heat. Add the red pepper flakes and asparagus pieces and cook for about 2 minutes, stirring continuously, or until the asparagus can just be pierced with a sharp knife.

Add the garlic and continue stirring for another 30 seconds. Add the soy sauce and sesame oil and stir for another 30 seconds. Serve immediately.

MOM TIP 1
▼

Sesame oil is an expensive,
flavorful oil made from sesame seeds.
Small bottles are usually available
in the Asian food section
of the supermarket

MOM TIP 2
▼

Another way to trim asparagus
is to bend the bottom of the stalk
until it snaps off. Discard the
tough, fibrous end.

MOM TIP 3
▼

Stir-Fried Asparagus
can be used as a topping for
cooked pasta.

Speedy Zucchini

SERVES: 4

Serve with: Sweet-and-Sour Meatballs (page 198) ▼ Preparation Time: 10 minutes

Cooking Time: 3-5 minutes ▼ Rating: Very Easy ▼ Can Prepare the Day Before: Yes

No ONE'S GOING TO REQUEST ZUCCHINI for a final meal. But that doesn't mean it's not a worthy vegetable, especially if it's flavored with garlic. And if you're making a big dinner, it's nice to have one dish that takes only five minutes to cook.

4 medium zucchini (see Mom Tip 1)
2 garlic cloves
2 tablespoons olive oil
½ teaspoon dried basil
  Dash salt
  Dash black pepper

Wash the zucchini and trim off and discard the ends. Cut the zucchini into ½-inch-thick rounds. Peel and finely chop the garlic.

Heat the oil in a large frying pan over medium-high heat. Add the garlic and basil and cook for about 30 seconds, or until the garlic begins to sizzle. Add the zucchini and stir. Turn down the heat to medium-low and cook for about 3 minutes for crisp zucchini; for softer zucchini, cook for 5 minutes, or until they can easily be pierced with a fork.

Season with the salt and pepper and serve.

MOM TIP 1

▼

Yellow squash can be substituted for
zucchini. Or if you want to make a
more colorful dish, use 2 zucchini
and 2 yellow squash.

MOM TIP 2

▼

To vary the flavor, add a tomato,
cut into ½-inch pieces, when you add
the zucchini to the pan. Or add a
few sprigs of washed, dried and
trimmed fresh cilantro, cut into
¼-inch pieces, just
before serving.

Gingery Carrots

SERVES: 4

Serve with: Hungarian Goulash (page 194) ▼ Preparation Time: 10 minutes

Cooking Time: 10 minutes ▼ Rating: Very Easy ▼ Can Prepare the Day Before: Yes

CARROTS MIGHT NOT GET YOUR GUESTS EXCITED. More than likely, they're burdened with memories of the institutional boiled-to-death kind. But when you add ginger and don't overcook them, you reinvent the carrot.

4 large carrots (see Mom Tip)

½ cup water

2 tablespoons butter or margarine

1 tablespoon sugar

½ teaspoon ground ginger

1 tablespoon lemon juice

Dash salt

Dash black pepper

Peel the carrots and slice into ½-inch-thick rounds. Put them in a medium pot, add the water, cover and bring to a boil. Turn down the heat to medium, cover and cook for about 8 minutes, or until the carrots can just be pierced with a sharp knife. Don't let them get too soft unless you like mushy carrots. Drain off any excess water but leave the carrots in the pot.

Add the butter or margarine to the carrots, stir and cook over medium heat for about 1 minute, or until the butter or margarine has melted. Add the sugar and ginger, stir and continue cooking for about 1 minute, or until the sugar has dissolved and the sugar mixture looks shiny.

Remove from the heat. Add the lemon juice, salt and pepper and serve.

Mom Tip

▼

To eliminate having to peel the carrots, substitute
peeled baby carrots, which are available in 1-pound bags.
Allow 3 to 4 carrots per person, either cutting them into
½-inch-thick rounds or leaving them whole.
Whole baby carrots will take 1 to 2
minutes longer to cook.

Gujerati Beans

SERVES: 4

Serve with: Chicken Satay with Peanut Sauce (page 220) ▼ Preparation Time: 10 minutes

Cooking Time: 8 minutes ▼ Rating: Very Easy ▼ Can Prepare the Day Before: Yes

GUJERATI BEANS ARE AN East INDIAN VARIATION of green beans. Gujerati refers to a region in India, although it sounds like a sports car from Bombay. My sister loves cooking these beans for dinner parties. I suspect she just likes saying the name.

1	pound fresh green beans
4	garlic cloves
2	tablespoons olive oil or corn oil
½	teaspoon sugar
¼	teaspoon red pepper flakes (½ teaspoon if you like spicy food)
¼	teaspoon black pepper
2	teaspoons mustard seeds (see Mom Tip)

Half-fill a medium pot with water, cover and begin heating over high heat.

Wash the beans. Snap ¼ inch off each end and pull; if a string comes off, throw it away with the ends. Cut the beans into ½-inch lengths.

When the water is boiling, add the beans. Boil, uncovered, for about 5 minutes, or until the beans have just begun to soften but are still slightly crisp.

Meanwhile, peel and finely chop the garlic.

When the beans are done, drain them in a colander and run cold water over them so that they stop cooking. Drain again and set aside.

Heat the oil in a large frying pan over medium-high heat. Add the garlic, sugar, red pepper flakes and pepper and cook for about 30 seconds, or until the garlic begins to sizzle. Add the mustard seeds and stir for about 15 seconds, or until they get hot and start to pop out of the pan. Add the beans and continue cooking for another 2 minutes, stirring occasionally, or until the beans are heated through and coated with the spices. Serve immediately, or set aside and reheat when needed.

MOM TIP

▼

Mustard seeds are packaged in glass bottles or
plastic packets and can be found with the other spices.
Powdered and prepared mustards are
not good substitutes.

Spicy Asian Baby Bok Choy

SERVES: 4

Serve with: Grilled Salmon (page 250) ▼ Preparation Time: 20 minutes

Cooking Time: 6 minutes ▼ Rating: Very Easy ▼ Can Prepare the Day Before: Yes

EVERY FOURTH OF JULY, we have a family cookout with the same family friends. To keep the event interesting, my mom likes to alter the menu slightly. After all, that's easier than making new friends. Last year, she asked me to provide a vegetable, and in honor of Hong Kong's reverting to Chinese rule, I made this one. It's not your typical patriotic dish, but it spiced up the evening.

1	teaspoon sesame seeds (see Mom Tip 1)
1	1-inch piece fresh ginger (see Mom Tip 2, page 197)
	or 1 teaspoon ground ginger
1	tablespoon peanut oil or corn oil
⅛	teaspoon red pepper flakes
2	tablespoons dry white wine
2	tablespoons soy sauce
1	teaspoon sesame oil (see Mom Tip 1, page 143)
1	teaspoon sugar
8	baby bok choy (see Mom Tip 2)
½	cup water

Put the sesame seeds in a small dry frying pan and heat over medium-high heat, stirring continually, for about 3 minutes, or until they begin to turn light brown. Remove from the heat and set aside.

If you are using fresh ginger, peel and finely chop it.

Heat the oil in a small pot over medium heat. Add the fresh or ground ginger and red pepper flakes and cook, stirring frequently, for 30 seconds. Add the wine, soy sauce, sesame oil and sugar and bring to a boil. Remove from the heat and set aside.

Cut each baby bok choy lengthwise in half and rinse thoroughly, making sure to get out the dirt between the leaves. Trim the stalk ends slightly but try to keep all the leaves attached to the stalks. Lay the bok choy in a single layer in a large frying pan. Add the water, cover and bring to a boil over medium-high heat. Turn down the heat to medium and cook for about 2 minutes, or until a sharp knife enters a stalk with just a little resistance. The leaves will have wilted. Immediately drain and transfer to a bowl.

Pour the sauce over the top, sprinkle with the toasted sesame seeds and serve. This dish can also be served cold.

Mom Tip 1

▼

Sesame seeds are usually available in the spice section of the supermarket. Toasting brings out their flavor.

Mom Tip 2

▼

Baby bok choy is the junior version of bok choy, a large Chinese cabbage. The baby version is 4 to 6 inches long and has anywhere from 4 to 8 leaves on celerylike stalks. When cooked, it shrinks considerably. It's usually available with the other fresh vegetables. If you can find only regular bok choy, which has leaves about 12 inches long, separate the leaves and wash thoroughly. Trim off and discard the bottom inch of the stalks and cut the rest into 1-inch-wide slices. Cook as directed above.

Grilled Vegetable Kebabs

SERVES: 4 (2 SKEWERS PER PERSON)

Serve with: Grilled Salmon (page 250) ▼ Preparation Time: 20 minutes

Cooking Time: 6-8 minutes ▼ Rating: Easy ▼ Can Prepare the Day Before: No

BARBECUING IS A GOOD WAY to cook lots of different vegetables at once. It's not worth lighting the grill just for vegetable kebabs, but once the coals are going for other foods, nothing could be easier. Just stick the veggies onto skewers.

CHOOSE 4 OR 5 FROM THE FOLLOWING:

8	cherry tomatoes
8	medium mushrooms
2	medium zucchini
2	large scallions
4	fat asparagus spears
1	large onion
1	medium potato
1	red bell pepper
1	green bell pepper
1	ear corn

8	metal or wooden skewers (see Mom Warning)
	Olive oil (see Mom Tip)
½	teaspoon salt
¼	teaspoon black pepper

Wash and dry any vegetable that doesn't need to be peeled. Cut away and discard the bottom ¼ inch of the mushroom stems. Remove and discard any stems from the cherry tomatoes. Trim off and discard any white part from the bottom of each asparagus stalk, usually 1 to 2 inches. Cut the asparagus stalks and scallions in half. Trim off the ends of the zucchini and discard. Cut off the root tip and the top 2 inches of the green parts of the scallions and discard.

Peel the onion and cut it into quarters. Separate the layers. Peel the potato and cut it into ¼-inch-thick slices. Cut the bell peppers in half, remove and discard the stems and seeds and cut them into 1-inch squares. Husk the corn and cut the cob into 1-inch rounds.

Thread the vegetables onto the skewers, leaving ¼ inch between each piece. (Thread the potato slices so that they will lie flat on the grill rack.) Put the skewers on a cookie sheet and spoon or brush some oil over the vegetables.

Prepare the grill as described on page 23, with the rack 6 inches from the heat source.

Place the skewers on the grill rack and grill for 3 to 4 minutes. Turn the skewers over and grill for another 3 to 4 minutes, or until the vegetables have become somewhat limp and the edges are charred. Remove them from the grill, season with the salt and pepper and serve immediately. Leftovers are good cold, on their own or added to a salad.

MOM TIP

▼

If you want a fancier flavoring than olive oil, use Easy Italian Dressing (see page 109).

MOM WARNING

▼

To prevent wooden skewers from catching fire on the grill, soak them in water for 30 minutes before using. Packages of wooden skewers are usually available in the gadget section of the grocery store.

Onion and Leek Curry

SERVES: 4

Serve with: Tandoori Chicken (page 231) ▼ Preparation Time: 20 minutes

Cooking Time: 20 minutes ▼ Rating: Easy ▼ Can Prepare the Day Before: Yes

Y EARS AGO, my parents came across this Indian dish at an English dinner party hosted by a beatnik saxophonist who was dating my baby-sitter. Amidst bongo playing and readings by the kooky beret-wearing guests, my mom and dad were served this curry. Proving she was a square, my mom asked for the recipe.

2	large leeks
1	large onion
1	garlic clove
2	tablespoons olive oil
2	whole cloves
1	bay leaf
1	teaspoon chili powder
½	teaspoon ground cumin
½	teaspoon ground coriander
½	teaspoon ground ginger
¼	teaspoon black pepper
¼	teaspoon ground cinnamon
1	8-ounce can tomato sauce

Wash the leeks (see Mom Tip 1, page 71). Trim ½ inch from the root end and at least 2 inches from the green end, or more if the leeks are wilted or dried out. Cut the leeks into ¼-inch half slices. Peel and thinly slice the onion. Peel and finely chop the garlic. Set aside.

Heat the oil in a large pot over medium-high heat. Add the cloves, bay leaf, chili powder, cumin, coriander, ginger, pepper and cinnamon and cook for 30 seconds. Add the leeks, onion and garlic and cook, stirring occasionally, for 3 minutes, or until the vegetables begin to soften.

Add the tomato sauce, cover and cook for 5 minutes. Stir, turn down the heat to medium-low and continue cooking, covered, for another 10 minutes. Discard the bay leaf and cloves before serving. Serve hot or cold.

Mom Warning

▼

Spices, especially ground spices, do not last forever.
As soon as they are opened and exposed to air, they begin
to lose their flavor. By the end of a year, you'll probably want
to replace them. In India, cooks often grind the amount
of spices they need every day. Don't buy huge containers
of any ground spice, unless you use it every day.

Pasta and Vegetarian Main Dishes

NOWHERE IS THE DIFFERENCE between cooking for yourself and cooking for company more pronounced than with pasta. When I'm making a meal for myself and my wife Jody, it's spaghetti. When people come over, it's pasta. Gone are the meatballs, and in comes Penne Arrabbiata or Tortellini with Creamy Tomato Sauce.

Pasta that's been painstakingly molded into individual letters is considered food for kids. That seems wrong. But even I can't serve my friends Spaghettios. Perhaps Fettucinnios for my swankier guests.

Since Jody and several people we know are vegetarians, it's important for us to have lots of options. We've included some other substantial vegetable dishes here, too, that I, a hopeless carnivore, can eat happily without feeling like I've been cheated out of a meal.

▲

Recipes

▼

Angel Hair Pasta with Tomatoes and Basil

SERVES: 4

Serve with: Prosciutto and Melon (page 58) ▼ Preparation Time: 15 minutes

Cooking Time: 2-6 minutes ▼ Rating: Very Easy ▼ Can Prepare the Day Before: No

THIS RECIPE IS ONLY SLIGHTLY MORE COMPLICATED than opening a jar of Ragù, but it will make your friends think you're Wolfgang Puck. There's no reason you have to break a sweat in the kitchen. The less that cooking feels like an hour on the StairMaster, the better. Save your energy for after-dinner speaking.

1 cup loosely packed fresh basil leaves or 1 tablespoon dried

3 garlic cloves

3 ounces fresh goat cheese; see Mom Tip 1 (optional)

2 tablespoons olive oil

½ teaspoon salt

¼ teaspoon black pepper

2 extra-large tomatoes, or two 15-ounce cans ready-cut tomatoes

16 ounces dried or fresh angel hair pasta or vermicelli (see Mom Tip 2)

Fill a large pot with water, cover and begin heating over high heat. (You can speed up the process by using hot water to start with.) While you're waiting for the water to come to a boil (5 to 10 minutes), start making the sauce.

Wash the fresh basil leaves, pat them dry between paper towels and cut them into ½-inch pieces.

Peel and finely chop the garlic. If using the goat cheese, cut it into ½-inch-thick slices. Put these ingredients in a large bowl, then add the oil, salt and pepper.

Peel the fresh tomatoes (see Mom Tip 3) and cut them into ½-inch chunks. Or if you are using canned tomatoes, drain off the liquid and save it for another use. Add the tomatoes to the bowl and mix thoroughly.

When the water comes to a boil, add the pasta and set the timer for 6 minutes (or 2 minutes, if using fresh angel hair pasta). Stir once or twice to keep the noodles from sticking together. When the timer rings, taste a noodle to see whether it's done. If it's a little too chewy, cook for another minute. Drain the noodles in a colander in the sink.

Transfer them to the bowl while they are still hot, toss them with the sauce and serve immediately. This dish is also good at room temperature.

MOM TIP 1

▼

Fresh goat cheese, which has a consistency similar to soft cream cheese but more flavor, melts quickly and will provide a creaminess to the sauce. Goat cheese is usually packaged in cylindrical shapes and is available in the gourmet-cheese department. Crumbled feta cheese can be substituted.

MOM TIP 2

▼

Angel hair pasta is the thinnest type of spaghetti. Vermicelli is almost as thin. Don't overcook it, or it will be mushy.

MOM TIP 3

▼

Here's an easy way to remove the skin from fresh tomatoes: drop them into the boiling pasta water for 30 seconds and transfer them to a bowl of cold water. Cut out and discard the core and pull away the skin. It should slip right off.

Pasta with Mushrooms and Artichokes

SERVES: 4

Serve with: Untraditional Matzo Ball Soup (page 86) ▼ Preparation Time: 20 minutes

Cooking Time: 15 minutes ▼ Rating: Very Easy ▼ Can Prepare the Day Before: No

COMBINING PASTA with both mushrooms and artichokes may sound unusual to you. It certainly did to me. My first thought when my mom gave me this recipe was, "I guess if I live long enough, I'll see pasta matched with everything." But mushrooms and artichokes work very well together.

1   6-ounce jar marinated artichoke hearts (see Mom Tip 1)

1   pound mushrooms

2   scallions

3   garlic cloves

¼   cup olive oil + more if needed

2   tablespoons chopped fresh parsley

⅛   teaspoon red pepper flakes

⅛   teaspoon black pepper
     Dash salt

¼   cup lemon juice

16   ounces farfalle (also called bow-tie or butterfly noodles; see Mom Tip 2)
     Grated Parmesan cheese (see Mom Tip 3, page 93)

Fill a large pot with water, cover and begin heating over high heat. (You can speed up the process by using hot water to start with.) While you're waiting for the water to come to a boil (5 to 10 minutes), make the sauce.

Lift the artichoke hearts from their marinade and cut each into 4 or 5 pieces. Set the marinade and artichokes aside.

Wash the mushrooms, cut away and discard the bottom ¼ inch of the stems and thinly slice the mushrooms. Wash the scallions. Cut off the root tip and the top 2 inches of the green parts and discard them. Cut the remaining white and green parts into ¼-inch pieces. Peel and finely chop the garlic.

Heat the ¼ cup oil in a large frying pan over medium-high heat. Add the mushrooms, scallions, garlic, parsley, red pepper flakes, pepper and salt and cook for about 5 minutes, stirring occasionally, until the vegetables begin to soften.

Remove from the heat, add the artichoke pieces and lemon juice and stir. If the vegetable mixture looks very dry, add 1 to 2 tablespoons of the artichoke marinade or additional oil and stir. Discard the rest of the marinade. Set the sauce aside, covered to keep warm.

When the water comes to a boil, add the pasta and set the timer for 10 minutes. Stir once or twice to keep the noodles from sticking together. When the timer rings, taste a noodle to see whether it's done. If it's a little too chewy, cook for another minute. Drain the noodles in a colander in the sink.

Reheat the mushroom and artichoke sauce, if necessary. Transfer the noodles to a large bowl. Pour the sauce on top, sprinkle with Parmesan cheese and serve immediately.

MOM TIP 1

▼

You can also buy marinated artichoke hearts at the deli counter. Or you can substitute plain artichoke hearts, which are available canned or frozen. Use half the can or box for this recipe. If you use frozen artichoke hearts, cook them following the directions on the package.

MOM TIP 2

▼

Farfalle noodles are available in bags or boxes next to the dried spaghetti and other pastas. They look like miniature bow ties. They are well suited for this sauce, which is mostly vegetables and little liquid. Any pasta that is 1 to 2 inches long and at least ½ inch wide—including small shells, spirals (fusilli, rotini) and tubes (mostaccioli, penne)—can be used.

Penne Arrabbiata

SERVES: 4

Serve with: Greek Salad (page 94) ▼ Preparation Time: 10 minutes

Cooking Time: 30 minutes ▼ Rating: Easy ▼ Can Prepare the Day Before: Sauce, yes; penne, no

PASTA COMES IN SO MANY DIFFERENT SIZES AND SHAPES that you'd think there would be some variation in taste. But with my eyes shut, I can barely tell the difference between spaghetti, rigatoni, macaroni and fettuccine. Add penne to the list. Penne look like short quill pens—hence the name— and they are often served with a spicy tomato sauce (*arrabbiata* means "angry" in Italian). But if you substitute another shape of pasta, nobody will be mad.

1	28-ounce can ready-cut tomatoes
1	pound fresh mushrooms
3	garlic cloves
8	thin slices Italian dry salami; see Mom Tip 1 (optional)
12	ounces penne or mostaccioli pasta (see Mom Tip 2)
2	tablespoons olive oil
¼	teaspoon red pepper flakes (more if you like very spicy food)
¼	teaspoon black pepper
	Grated Parmesan cheese (see Mom Tip 3, page 93)

Fill a large pot with water, cover and begin heating over high heat. Meanwhile, make the sauce.

Put the tomatoes and their liquid in a medium pot and bring to a boil over high heat. Turn down the heat to medium-low and cook, uncovered, for 15 minutes, or until the tomato mixture is very thick. Stir occasionally to make sure the tomatoes aren't sticking to the bottom of the pot. Remove from the heat and set aside.

While the tomatoes are cooking, wash the mushrooms, cut away and discard the bottom ¼ inch of the stems and thinly slice the mushrooms. Peel and finely chop the garlic. Cut the salami into ¼-inch-thick strips, if using.

Add the noodles to the boiling water, stir so they don't stick together and set the timer for 12 minutes.

Heat the oil in a large frying pan over medium heat. Add the mushrooms, garlic, salami, red pepper flakes and pepper and cook for about 2 minutes, stirring occasionally, until the mushrooms begin to soften. Add the tomato mixture and stir thoroughly to prevent the salami strips from sticking together. Remove from the heat and cover to keep warm until the noodles are ready.

Stir the noodles occasionally to keep them from sticking together. When the timer rings, taste a noodle to see whether it's done. If it's a little too chewy, cook for another minute. Drain the noodles in a colander in the sink. Shake the colander to make sure all the water drains out.

Transfer the noodles to a large bowl. Pour the sauce on top, sprinkle with Parmesan cheese and serve immediately.

MOM TIP 1

▼

Italian dry salami is available
at the deli counter, sliced to order,
or sealed in plastic in the refrigerated
section near the cheese.

MOM TIP 2

▼

Penne and mostaccioli are thin
tubes of pasta about 1½ inches long.
They are available in boxes or plastic
bags alongside other dried pastas.
Fusilli, large shells, macaroni,
rotelle, rotini or ziti can
be substituted.

Tortellini with Creamy Tomato Sauce

SERVES: 4

Serve with: Broccoli, Avocado and Tomato Salad (page 98) ▼ Preparation Time: 5 minutes

Cooking Time: 20 minutes (10 minutes if using fresh tortellini)

Rating: Very Easy ▼ Can Prepare the Day Before: No (see Mom Warning)

IF I WERE A DEDICATED COOK, I'd spend half a day rolling out the tortellini dough, making a filling, stuffing it inside little squares and then twisting them up. But I'd as soon make my own clothes. I do open the bag myself, though.

Store-bought tortellini actually taste pretty good just sprinkled with Parmesan cheese, and I always keep a bag around for an easy meal. If you have a few extra minutes, the Creamy Tomato Sauce makes them worthy of serving to company.

4	garlic cloves
2	tablespoons olive oil
½	teaspoon red pepper flakes
1	15-ounce can tomato sauce
12	ounces dried tortellini (see Mom Tip)
½	cup whipping (not whipped) cream
	Dash salt
	Dash black pepper

Fill a large pot with water, cover and begin heating over high heat. (You can speed up the process by using hot water to start with.) While you're waiting for the water to come to a boil (5 to 10 minutes), make the sauce.

Peel and finely chop the garlic. Heat the oil in a large frying pan over medium-high heat. Add the garlic and red pepper flakes. After about 30 seconds, when the garlic begins to sizzle, add the tomato sauce. Stir and continue cooking for about 5 minutes, or until the sauce thickens slightly. Remove from the heat.

When the water comes to a boil, add the tortellini. Stir to make sure they are all submerged. Set the timer for 14 minutes (if using dried tortellini) or 4 minutes (if using fresh tortellini). Stir once or twice during the cooking to keep them from sticking together. When the timer rings, taste a tortellini to see whether it's done. If it's a little too chewy, cook for another minute. Drain the tortellini in a colander in the sink.

Reheat the tomato sauce. When it reaches a boil, add the cream and stir. Add the tortellini and stir again so that they are coated with sauce. Cook for another minute, but do not allow the sauce to boil. Season with the salt and pepper. Serve immediately.

MOM TIP
▼

Tortellini are small circles of pasta filled with meat or cheese and then pinched together to form rings. They look something like miniature bagels. Dried tortellini are sold in boxes, bags or loose at Italian delicatessens. They are also available fresh and frozen. Fresh and frozen tortellini take only 3 to 4 minutes to cook. Check the directions on the package for the exact time. To serve 4 people, you'll need at least 1 pound.

MOM WARNING
▼

If pasta sits in a sauce overnight, it will get soggy.

Spaghetti with Shrimp Sauce

SERVES: 4

Serve with: Caesar Salad (page 92)

Preparation Time: 20 minutes (using a food processor) or 25 minutes (by hand)

Cooking Time: 15 minutes ▼ Rating: Easy ▼ Can Prepare the Day Before: Sauce, yes; spaghetti, no

WHEN MY SISTER BONNIE brought home her first boyfriend in high school, my mom served spaghetti, figuring that everybody likes it. As my dad grilled him about his career prospects, the poor guy was nervously trying to remember how to use a fork. He must have spilled half the plate on his clip-on tie. As the younger brother, I delighted in the spectacle. But when I serve spaghetti now, I speak in calming tones so that everyone can concentrate on the delicate process of fork twirling.

This sauce is an innovative use of shrimp. I used to think that any shrimp which wasn't in shrimp cocktail was a wasted shrimp. But this recipe proves it's more versatile than I thought. And since the sauce is clumpy instead of runny, there should be a lot fewer stains on your guests' shirts.

1	small onion
6	garlic cloves
¼	cup fresh parsley leaves
1½	pounds cooked shrimp (see Mom Tip 1)
¼	cup olive oil
½	cup fresh bread crumbs (see Mom Tip 2)
2	tablespoons ketchup
½	teaspoon black pepper
16	ounces spaghetti
3	tablespoons lemon juice
	Hot pepper sauce (optional)

Fill a large pot with water, cover and begin heating over high heat. (You can speed up the process by using hot water to start with.) While you're waiting for the water to come to a boil (5 to 10 minutes), make the sauce.

Peel the onion and cut it into quarters. Peel the garlic. Wash the parsley and pat it dry between paper towels. Cut off and discard the stems.

With a food processor: Put the onion, garlic and parsley into the appliance bowl and process for about 10 seconds, or until finely chopped. Remove from the bowl and set aside. Put the shrimp into the bowl and process for about 10 seconds, or until finely chopped. Set aside.

By hand: Finely chop the onion, garlic and parsley. Set aside. Finely chop the shrimp and set aside.

Heat 2 tablespoons of the oil in a large frying pan over medium-high heat. Add the onion-parsley mixture and cook for about 5 minutes, or until it begins to soften. Add the shrimp, bread crumbs, ketchup and pepper and stir to mix thoroughly. Remove from the heat and set aside.

When the water comes to a boil, add the spaghetti. Stir to make sure all the noodles are submerged. Set the timer for 8 minutes. Continue to stir every minute or two to keep them from sticking together. When the timer rings, taste a noodle to see whether it's done. If it's a little too chewy, cook for another minute. Drain the noodles in a colander in the sink.

A few minutes before the noodles are ready, reheat the shrimp sauce over medium heat (see Mom Warning). Add the lemon juice and hot pepper sauce to taste, if desired, and stir thoroughly.

Transfer the drained noodles to a large bowl. Add the remaining 2 tablespoons oil and toss the noodles to coat each strand (the shrimp sauce is not "saucy"). Distribute the noodles on plates and top with the sauce.

MOM TIP 1

▼

Since the shrimp will be chopped, the cheapest (which are often the smallest) will do. I usually use already cooked and peeled baby shrimp, which are about the size of my thumbnail and are available fresh or frozen in my grocery store. However, if you can't find them, any shrimp will do.

Another economical way to buy shrimp is frozen in plastic bags at the grocery store. The shrimp may be raw or cooked and shelled or still in the shell. Defrost them by immersing them in boiling water for about 30 seconds. If they are raw, continue cooking them for 3 to 5 minutes, depending on their size, until they are pink and firm, not mushy. Peel if necessary.

MOM TIP 2

▼

If you have a blender or food processor, it's easy to make fresh bread crumbs. Cut 1 slice of good-quality bread into quarters and process for about 10 seconds, or until it is finely chopped. One slice of sandwich bread makes about ½ cup crumbs. Or you can pull the bread into tiny pieces with your fingers.

MOM WARNING

▼

Don't let the sauce cook for more than 1 minute after you've added the shrimp, or they will get tough.

Black Bean Lasagna

SERVES: 8

Serve with: Southwestern Coleslaw (page 100) ▼ Preparation Time: 45 minutes

Cooking Time: 40-45 minutes (70-75 minutes if refrigerated)

Rating: Not So Easy ▼ Can Prepare the Day Before: Yes

MY GRANDMA MADE THIS VEGETARIAN-STYLE LASAGNA for my wife Jody's bridal shower. No men were allowed, which was perfectly fine with me. My dad, brother-in-law Tom and I had never been so eager to get out of the house. We went to see *Dumb and Dumber*. Unfortunately, the movie wasn't long enough, and the estrogen-fest hadn't broken up by the time we got back. We men huddled in the kitchen polishing off the leftover lasagna while the women continued. I will always be grateful to Black Bean Lasagna for giving me shelter from that storm.

While regular lasagna is a popular dish for serving the multitudes, this one may be even better, because very few people have had it.

1   8-ounce package cream cheese (see Mom Tip 1)

1   medium onion

2   garlic cloves

1   red or green bell pepper

¼   cup fresh cilantro sprigs (about 20)

1   tablespoon olive oil + 1 teaspoon for boiling noodles and more for greasing pan

2   16-ounce cans black beans (see Mom Warning, page 77)

1   29-ounce can tomato sauce

12   lasagna noodles (see Mom Tip 2)

1   16-ounce container cottage cheese

¼   cup sour cream

Take the cream cheese out of the refrigerator so that it will begin to soften.

If you're not using precooked noodles, fill a large pot with water, cover and begin heating over high heat. (You can speed up the process by using hot water to start with.) While you're waiting for the water to come to a boil (5 to 10 minutes), start making the sauce.

Peel the onion and cut it into ½-inch pieces. Peel and finely chop the garlic. Wash the bell pepper and cut it into ½-inch pieces. Wash the cilantro sprigs and pat them dry between paper towels. Cut off and discard the stems and cut the leafy parts into ½-inch pieces.

Heat the 1 tablespoon olive oil in a large frying pan over medium heat. Add the onion, garlic, bell pepper and cilantro and cook for about 5 minutes, stirring occasionally, until the vegetables have softened.

While the vegetables are cooking, drain the beans, discarding the liquid, and rinse them in a strainer or colander under cold running water.

Add half the beans to the onion mixture. Mash the other half with a fork and add them to the mixture. Add the tomato sauce and continue cooking, stirring occasionally, for another 5 minutes, or until the mixture has thickened. Remove from the heat and set aside.

When the water comes to a boil, add the 1 teaspoon oil (see Mom Tip 3). Add the lasagna noodles one at a time, pushing them gently into the water until they are fully submerged. Set the timer for 12 minutes. Stir occasionally to keep them from sticking together. When the timer rings, taste a corner of a noodle to see whether it's done. If it's a little too chewy, cook for another minute. Drain the noodles in a colander in the sink, running cold water over them to stop the cooking. Separate any that have stuck together and set aside.

Mix the cream cheese, cottage cheese and sour cream in a large bowl and set aside.

If you plan to bake the lasagna now, begin heating the oven to 350 degrees.

Rub the bottom and sides of an 8-x-12-inch or 9-x-13-inch baking pan with oil. Cover the bottom of the pan with 4 lasagna noodles, overlapping them slightly. Cover the noodles with one-third of the bean sauce, spreading it evenly, then cover the bean mixture with one-third of the cheese mixture. Add another layer of 4 noodles, another one-third of the bean sauce and another one-third of the cheese mixture. Then add the remaining 4 noodles, bean sauce and cheese mixture.

Cover the pan with aluminum foil and seal it tightly around the edges. At this stage, you can refrigerate the lasagna and cook it the next day.

Bake the lasagna, covered, for 40 to 45 minutes (1 hour and 10 minutes to 1 hour and 15 minutes if it is coming straight from the refrigerator), or until the sauce is bubbling and the cheese is browned. Serve immediately, or reduce the oven temperature to 200 degrees and keep warm for up to 1 hour.

Mom Tip 1

▼

Whenever you see cream cheese listed as an ingredient, you will usually have to combine it with other ingredients, which means the softer it is, the better. So remove it from the refrigerator up to a few hours ahead of time to allow it to reach room temperature. If the cream cheese is still too firm, cut it into 1-inch pieces before combining it with the other ingredients.

Mom Tip 2

▼

One of the tedious parts of making lasagna is cooking the noodles, so if you can find boxes of precooked dried or "no-boil" noodles, buy them. They need no cooking. Just lay them in the pan as directed above. They will soften during baking and taste just like regular lasagna noodles—even better, in my opinion, because they're not as thick. Use as many as needed to make complete layers.

Mom Tip 3

▼

The oil stays on the surface and coats each piece of pasta as it goes into the water, thus helping prevent the noodles from sticking to each other.

Lasagna

SERVES: 8-10

Serve with: Bruschetta (page 60) ▼ Preparation Time: 1¼ hours
Cooking Time: 1 hour (1½ hours if refrigerated) ▼ Rating: Not So Easy
Can Prepare the Day Before: Yes

LIKE THE OLD FAMILY DOG who's learned to take the pokes in the eye and pulling of the tail, lasagna is very forgiving. It's a perfect dinner-party food because it's easier than preparing a smorgasbord, it serves up to 10 people, and most people like it. It's also cheap.

I made this lasagna for my first dinner party, entertaining Jody's colleagues, all overworked interns. They were easy to impress because they hadn't had a home-cooked meal in months. And like businesses that save their first dollar bill, I will always have the place mat with the lasagna stains from that night. Maybe I should frame it and hang it next to Jody's med school diploma.

MEAT SAUCE

2 medium onions

3 garlic cloves

2 pounds lean ground beef

1 15-ounce can ready-cut tomatoes

1 12-ounce can tomato paste + 1 can water + more if necessary
   (see Mom Tip 1)

2 bay leaves

1 teaspoon dried parsley

1 teaspoon dried oregano

1 teaspoon salt

½ teaspoon black pepper

NOODLES

1   teaspoon corn oil or vegetable oil

12   lasagna noodles (see Mom Tips 1 and 2, page 171)

CHEESE SAUCE

3   tablespoons butter or margarine

3   tablespoons all-purpose flour

2   cups milk

1   8-ounce container cottage cheese (see Mom Tip 2)

1   cup grated mozzarella cheese (4 ounces)

¼   cup grated Parmesan cheese

If you're not using precooked noodles, fill a large pot with water, cover and begin heating over high heat. (You can speed up the process by using hot water to start with.) While you're waiting for the water to come to a boil (5 to 10 minutes), start making the meat sauce.

MEAT SAUCE: Peel the onions and cut them into ½-inch pieces. Peel and finely chop the garlic. Set aside.

Brown the beef, without adding any oil, in a large frying pan or medium pot over medium heat, stirring frequently to break it into small clumps, about 10 minutes. After the meat has browned, drain off any fat by covering the pan almost completely with a lid and carefully pouring the liquid into an empty can. Discard the can.

Add the onions, garlic, tomatoes and their liquid, tomato paste and water, bay leaves, parsley, oregano, salt and pepper and stir thoroughly. Cover and cook over low heat for 30 minutes. Stir every 10 minutes and add up to ½ cup more water if the sauce seems too thick. Remove and discard the bay leaves and set aside.

NOODLES: When the water comes to a boil, add the oil to the water (see Mom Tip 3, page 171). Add the lasagna noodles one at a time, pushing them gently into the water until they are fully submerged. Set the timer for 12 minutes. Stir occasionally to keep them from sticking together. When the timer rings, taste a corner of a noodle to see whether it's done. If it's a little too chewy, cook for another minute.

Drain the noodles in a colander in the sink, running cold water over them to stop the cooking. Separate any that have stuck together and set aside.

CHEESE SAUCE: Melt the butter or margarine in a medium pot over medium-high heat. When it has melted, add the flour and stir until it is completely absorbed. Add the milk and cook, stirring continually, for about 3 minutes, or until the mixture thickens. Turn the heat to low, add the cottage cheese, mozzarella cheese and Parmesan cheese and stir until they melt, about 5 minutes. Remove from the heat and set aside.

If you plan to bake the lasagna now, begin preheating the oven to 350 degrees.

To assemble: Put ½ cup meat sauce in an 8-x-12-inch or 9-x-13-inch baking pan and shake the pan so the sauce spreads around. Don't worry if it doesn't completely cover the bottom. Lay 4 noodles on top of the sauce, overlapping them slightly. Cover the noodles with 2 cups meat sauce, spreading it evenly. Cover the meat sauce with ½ cup cheese sauce. Continue adding two more layers of noodles, meat sauce and cheese sauce, ending with the layer of cheese sauce.

Cover the pan with aluminum foil and seal it tightly around the edges. At this stage, you can refrigerate the lasagna and cook it the next day.

Bake the lasagna, covered, for 45 minutes (1 hour and 15 minutes if it is coming straight from the refrigerator). Remove the foil and cook for an additional 15 minutes, or until the cheese topping begins to brown. Serve immediately, or reduce the oven temperature to 200 degrees and keep warm for up to 1 hour.

MOM TIP 1

▼

Lasagna is pretty hard to ruin
unless you burn it, so the proportions
of the ingredients can vary. If you
prefer lasagna that firmly holds its
shape when you cut it into squares,
use the whole 1-pound box of noodles
instead of the 12 called for and use
more noodles in each layer.
If you like juicy lasagna that is served
in a soup bowl, use the number
of noodles called for in the recipe
but add ½ cup extra water
to the meat sauce.

MOM TIP 2

▼

To keep the amount of
fat down, use low-fat or
nonfat cottage cheese.

Cheese Fondue

SERVES: 4-6

Serve with: Spinach and Strawberry Salad (page 96) ▼ Preparation Time: 15 minutes

Cooking Time: 20 minutes ▼ Rating: Not So Easy ▼ Can Prepare the Day Before: No

Jody and I discovered cheese fondue on our honeymoon in London. We shared a booth in a dark restaurant, eating cheese-dipped bread by the light of the fondue flame. It was so good that we ate way too much, and we had to sit in the restaurant for two hours while the food settled. Very romantic—except for the stomachache.

When we returned to America to start our life together, we told my parents about this great new food that would soon be all the rage. They laughed and told us about a long-forgotten time they called "The Sixties," when fondue was popular. After some searching, we did find a fondue pot in a department store. One of the older salespeople knew what we were talking about. Since then, we've enjoyed initiating our friends. We have to warn them to stop before they eat too much.

1	loaf French bread (at least 2 feet long)
1¼	pounds Gouda cheese (see Mom Tip 1)
2	teaspoons lemon juice
1½	tablespoons cornstarch
1	cup dry white wine (such as Chardonnay or Chenin Blanc)
⅛	teaspoon black pepper
⅛	teaspoon ground nutmeg

Set up the fondue pot frame and burner attachment on the table and prepare but do not light the burner (see Mom Tip 2, page 283). If you have fondue forks (extralong forks with heatproof handles), set them out. You can also use regular forks, metal skewers or chopsticks.

Cut the bread into 1-inch cubes, making sure at least one side of each cube is crust. Pile the cubes into a bowl and set on the table.

Grate the cheese on a large-hole grater (see Mom Tip 2). Set aside. Combine the lemon juice and cornstarch in a small cup, stir thoroughly until smooth and set aside.

Add the wine to the fondue pot and begin heating it on the stove over medium-high heat. When it begins to bubble around the edges, add the grated cheese a little at a time, stirring continually with a wooden spoon until all of it has melted. When the mixture begins to boil, add the pepper, nutmeg and lemon-juice mixture. Continue cooking and stirring until the mixture thickens, about 5 minutes.

Light the fondue burner. Set the fondue pot on the pot frame over the burner. Call the guests. Encourage them to stir the cheese when they dip their bread into the pot.

MOM TIP 1
▼

Gouda cheese can be found in the gourmet cheese section. It is usually covered with a coating of red wax for protection. Remove and discard the wax and any other visible waxy coating underneath.

MOM TIP 2
▼

If you don't have a grater, you can use a potato peeler to peel the cheese into long, thin strips. You can also grate cheese quickly in a food processor, using the shredding blade.

MOM WARNING
▼

Don't drink iced liquids while you're eating cheese fondue, or you'll feel as if you swallowed a bowling ball. Wine is the preferred beverage.

Mushroom Turnover

SERVES: 4

Serve with: Russian Vegetable Borscht (page 74) ▼ Preparation Time: 45 minutes

Cooking Time: 30-35 minutes ▼ Rating: Not So Easy ▼ Can Prepare the Day Before: No

Mushroom Turnover isn't a side order of mushrooms. It's a good way to make a substantial main dish out of a simple vegetable. I always feel a little sheepish about buying "puff pastry." It's not exactly a guy thing.

Once you've got it, though, this is a pretty easy recipe. Be prepared, because it puffs up more than you'd think. It goes into the oven looking like a pancake but comes out looking like a throw pillow.

1	17-ounce package frozen puff pastry sheets (see Mom Tip 1)
1½	cups cooked rice (or ½ cup uncooked rice)
5	scallions
1	pound medium or large mushrooms (see Mom Tip 2)
1	tablespoon butter or margarine
½	cup sour cream
4	teaspoons dried dill
½	teaspoon salt
¼	teaspoon black pepper

Thaw the puff pastry sheets at room temperature for 30 minutes before gently unfolding them. While waiting for them to thaw, prepare the filling.

If you don't have leftover rice, cook as follows: add 1 cup water to a medium pot, cover and bring to a boil over high heat. Add the rice, return the water to a boil, stir, cover, and turn the heat to low. Cook for 15 minutes and then remove from the heat. Leave covered until needed.

Wash the scallions. Cut off the root tip and top 2 inches of the green parts and discard them. Cut the remaining white and green parts into ¼-inch pieces. Wash the mushrooms and cut away and discard the bottom ¼ inch of the stems. Cut medium mushrooms into quarters, large mushrooms into eighths.

Place an oven rack in the middle position and begin preheating the oven to 400 degrees.

Heat the butter or margarine in a large frying pan over medium heat. Add the scallions and mushrooms and cook, stirring occasionally, for about 10 minutes, until the vegetables are very soft. Remove from the heat and drain off and discard any liquid in the pan.

Add the mushroom mixture to the rice. Add the sour cream, dill, salt and pepper and mix thoroughly. Set aside.

Gently unfold 1 puff pastry sheet and place it on an ungreased cookie sheet. Spread the rice mixture over the puff pastry in an even layer, leaving a ½-inch border.

Gently unfold the other puff pastry sheet and lay it on top of the rice mixture. Carefully pinch the 2 puff pastry sheets together on all edges so that the filling won't leak out.

Bake for 30 to 35 minutes, or until the pastry layers have puffed up and the top is golden brown. Cut into quarters and serve immediately, or let cool slightly and serve warm.

MOM TIP 1

▼

Puff pastry sheets come 2 to
a box and are available in the
frozen food section.

MOM TIP 2

▼

The larger the mushrooms,
the fewer you have to wash.
On the other hand, large mushrooms
often cost more. It's time
versus money.

Eggplant Parmesan

SERVES: 4 AS A MAIN COURSE, 8 AS A SIDE DISH

Serve with: Broccoli, Avocado and Tomato Salad (page 98) ▼ Preparation Time: 35 minutes

Cooking Time: 50-55 minutes ▼ Rating: Not So Easy ▼ Can Prepare the Day Before: Yes

I'M A CONFIRMED CARNIVORE who feels that any dish without meat is an appetizer. But Eggplant Parmesan is substantial enough to count as meat. What's great about eggplant is you don't have to take out the bones and you don't have to remove the skin. This dish is hearty enough for a meat eater, but made for a vegetarian.

	SAUCE (see Mom Tip)
1	small onion
2	garlic cloves
4-6	tablespoons olive oil
1	15-ounce can ready-cut tomatoes
1	teaspoon sugar
1	teaspoon dried basil
½	teaspoon salt
¼	teaspoon black pepper
1	large eggplant (see Mom Tips 1 and 2, page 183)
2	cups grated mozzarella cheese (8 ounces)
½	cup grated Parmesan cheese

Preheat the oven to 400 degrees.

SAUCE: Peel the onion and cut it into ½-inch pieces. Peel and finely chop the garlic.

Heat 2 tablespoons of the oil in a medium pot over medium heat. Add the onion and garlic and cook for about 5 minutes, stirring occasionally, until they begin to soften. Add the tomatoes and their liquid, sugar, basil, salt and pepper and cook, uncovered, stirring occasionally, for about 15 minutes, until you have a thick tomato sauce. Remove from the heat and set aside.

While the sauce is cooking, wash the eggplant, trim off and discard the ends and cut it lengthwise into ¼-inch-thick slices.

Heat 2 tablespoons of the oil in a large frying pan over medium-high heat. Add as many slices of eggplant as will fit in a single layer and cook for about 2 minutes, or until they begin to brown on the bottom (see Mom Warning). Turn them over, press them down with a metal spatula to squeeze out some of the oil they have absorbed and cook for another 2 minutes, or until they begin to brown on the bottom. Turn down the heat to medium if the eggplant starts to burn. Transfer the cooked slices to a plate and repeat until all the eggplant is cooked, adding up to 2 more tablespoons oil to the pan.

Put ¼ cup tomato sauce in a medium casserole or baking dish and shake it to spread the sauce around. Don't worry if the sauce doesn't completely cover the bottom. Lay half the eggplant slices on top of the sauce. It's best if it's in a single layer, but make a double layer if necessary. Spread half the remaining tomato sauce on top of the eggplant. Scatter half the mozzarella cheese over the tomato sauce. Sprinkle on ¼ cup of the Parmesan cheese. Add a second layer of eggplant, tomato sauce, mozzarella cheese and Parmesan cheese.

Bake, uncovered, for 30 to 35 minutes, or until the sauce bubbles and the top begins to brown. Serve immediately, or let cool slightly and serve warm.

MOM TIP
▼

If you're in a hurry, use a 16-ounce jar of spaghetti sauce instead of making your own tomato sauce.

MOM WARNING
▼

Eggplant likes oil and will happily absorb several cups if you let it. Don't, unless you're on a weight-gaining diet. Add only 1 to 2 tablespoons of oil with each batch of eggplant you cook. Pressing on the eggplant slices with a spatula helps release some of the oil they've already absorbed.

Ratatouille

SERVES: 4 AS A MAIN COURSE WITH RICE, 8 AS A SIDE DISH

Serve with: Middle Eastern Bulgur Wheat Pilaf (page 130) ▼ Preparation Time: 20 minutes

Cooking Time: 40 minutes ▼ Rating: Easy ▼ Can Prepare the Day Before: Yes

RATATOUILLE IS A DISH FROM THE SOUTH OF FRANCE, a land of wine, nude beaches and eggplant. You could certainly enjoy Ratatouille naked and drunk, but that's not the right tone to set for a dinner party. Eggplant is the backbone of Ratatouille—and the workhorse of the vegetarian diet. I like eggplant, but not as much as my wife Jody does. I figure that when a person gives up meat, his or her taste for eggplant must grow more acute.

1	large onion
1	eggplant (about 1 pound; see Mom Tip 1)
1	red bell pepper
1	large zucchini
2	garlic cloves
3	tablespoons olive oil
1	15-ounce can ready-cut tomatoes
½	teaspoon salt
¼	teaspoon black pepper

Peel the onion and cut it into ½-inch pieces. Wash the eggplant and cut off and discard the stem. Cut the eggplant into ½-inch-thick slices, then cut the slices into ½-inch pieces. Wash the red bell pepper, cut it in half, remove and discard the stem and seeds and cut it into ½-inch pieces. Wash the zucchini, trim off and discard the ends and cut it into ¼-inch-thick slices. Peel and finely chop the garlic.

Heat the oil in a large pot over medium heat. Add the onion and cook for about 5 minutes, stirring occasionally, until it begins to soften. Add the eggplant and red bell pepper and continue cooking for another 5 minutes, stirring occasionally. The onion will be very soft and the other vegetables will have begun to soften.

Add the zucchini and garlic, stir and cook for another minute. Then add the tomatoes and their liquid, salt and pepper and stir again. Cover and cook for 20 minutes. Remove the lid and continue cooking for another 10 minutes, or until most of the liquid has evaporated. Serve immediately, or let cool and serve at room temperature. Ratatouille is also good cold.

MOM TIP 1

▼

Choose an eggplant that has shiny purple skin and no brown spots. There's no need to peel it. The white flesh starts to turn brown as soon as it's exposed to air, but that doesn't matter for Ratatouille.

MOM TIP 2

▼

I grew up hearing that you had to slice eggplants, sprinkle them with salt and let them drain in a colander for 30 minutes to get the bitter juices out before you cooked them. I tried that a few times, and it was such a nuisance, I decided to skip that step. It didn't seem to make any difference.

Spicy Lentils and Spinach

SERVES: 4

Serve with: Bruschetta (page 60) ▼ Preparation Time: 15 minutes

Cooking Time: 30 minutes ▼ Rating: Easy ▼ Can Prepare the Day Before: Partially

L ENTILS TASTE SURPRISINGLY GOOD, considering that in their uncooked state, they look and feel like the inside of a beanbag. According to my edition of the *Encyclopaedia Britannica*, they are "highly esteemed as green food for suckling ewes."

They've also been eaten by humans for over 5,000 years. When combined with spinach, they make a highly nutritious salad that can stand on its own. This one should be a hit at dinner parties, especially if anyone happens to bring a pet suckling ewe.

1	medium onion
2	garlic cloves
2	tablespoons olive oil
½	teaspoon salt
½	teaspoon ground cumin
½	teaspoon ground ginger
¼	teaspoon ground cinnamon
⅛	teaspoon red pepper flakes
2	tablespoons lemon juice
1	cup dried lentils (see Mom Tip 1)
3	cups water
1	6-ounce bag washed fresh spinach (see Mom Tip 2)

Peel the onion and cut it into ½-inch pieces. Peel and finely chop the garlic.

Heat the oil in a large frying pan over medium heat. Add the onion, garlic, salt, cumin, ginger, cinnamon and red pepper flakes and cook for about 5 minutes, stirring occasionally, until the onion begins to soften. Remove from the heat, add the lemon juice and set aside.

Rinse the lentils in a strainer and examine carefully to make sure no pebbles are included. Put the lentils and water in a medium pot and bring to a boil over high heat. Turn down the heat to low, cover and cook for 20 minutes. Test the lentils to see whether they're soft by tasting one. Undercooked lentils are like pebbles. If the lentils are too hard, cook for another 5 to 10 minutes. Drain the lentils and add them to the onion mixture. At this point, you can refrigerate the mixture overnight and complete the final step just before serving.

Cook the lentil mixture over medium heat for about 5 minutes, stirring occasionally, until it is hot throughout. Add half the spinach and stir until it begins to soften. Add the rest of the spinach and keep stirring until it softens. Serve immediately, or let cool slightly and serve warm.

Mom Tip 1

▼

Dried lentils, which are usually brownish green but sometimes orange, are packaged in 1-pound bags and are stocked next to the rice and dried beans.

Mom Tip 2

▼

Fresh spinach is usually available prewashed in plastic bags in the produce department. It's a lot easier to deal with than loose bunches of spinach, which are usually encrusted with dirt and require several soakings. Look for baby spinach, but if it's unavailable, use regular spinach, removing the long stems and tearing the leaves in half.

Stuffed Peppers

SERVES: 4

Serve with: Onion Focaccia (page 62) ▼ Preparation Time: 30 minutes

Cooking Time: 30-40 minutes ▼ Rating: Not So Easy ▼ Can Prepare the Day Before: Yes

THIS IS A VERY FLEXIBLE RECIPE. If you stuff the peppers with rice, sun-dried tomatoes and mint, it's Greek. If you stuff them with rice, spinach and curry powder, it's East Indian.

> 4 medium red, yellow or green bell peppers (see Mom Tip 1)
> Greek or Indian Filling
> Olive oil for greasing pan

Fill a large pot half-full with water, cover and begin heating over high heat.

Meanwhile, cut off the stem end of each bell pepper about ¼ inch from the top. Cut out and discard the stem itself. A thin circle of pepper will be left. Cut it up and reserve it for the filling, or save for another use. Remove the seeds and pull out and discard any white membranes inside the peppers.

When the water comes to a boil, immerse the peppers in the water, turn down the heat to medium, cover and cook for 10 minutes. The peppers will soften considerably. Remove them from the water and set them on a plate, upside down, to cool and drain. Discard the water.

Make one of the fillings (see next page).

Preheat the oven to 375 degrees. Lightly rub the bottom of a casserole or baking dish with oil.

Stand the peppers in the dish with their cavities facing up. If they don't stand firmly, slice a very thin layer from the bottom, being careful not to puncture the cavity. Spoon one-fourth of the filling into each pepper.

Cover the dish with aluminum foil and bake for about 30 minutes, or until the peppers are very hot and can easily be pierced with a knife. Serve immediately, or let cool and serve at room temperature.

GREEK FILLING

3	cups cooked rice (or 1 cup uncooked rice)
4	scallions
3	garlic cloves
6	sun-dried tomatoes (see Mom Tip 2)
¼	cup raisins
2	tablespoons olive oil
1	tablespoon dried mint
½	teaspoon salt
¼	teaspoon ground cinnamon
¼	teaspoon black pepper

If you don't have leftover rice, cook as follows: add 2 cups water to a medium pot, cover and bring to a boil over high heat. Add the rice, return the water to a boil, stir, cover and turn the heat to low. Cook for 15 minutes and then remove from the heat. Leave covered until needed.

Wash the scallions. Cut off the root tip and top 2 inches of the green parts and discard them. Cut the remaining white and green parts into ¼-inch pieces. Peel and finely chop the garlic. Slice the sun-dried tomatoes into ¼-inch slivers.

Combine the scallions, garlic, tomatoes, raisins, oil, mint, salt, cinnamon and pepper in a large bowl. Add the rice and mix thoroughly.

INDIAN FILLING

2	cups cooked rice (or ⅔ cup uncooked rice)
1	10-ounce package frozen chopped spinach
1	medium onion
3	garlic cloves
2	tablespoons olive oil
1	teaspoon curry powder
½	teaspoon salt

¼   teaspoon black pepper
¼   teaspoon ground turmeric

If you don't have leftover rice, cook as follows: add 1⅓ cups water to a medium pot, cover and bring to a boil over high heat. Add the rice, return the water to a boil, stir, cover and turn the heat to low. Cook for 15 minutes and then remove from the heat. Leave covered until needed.

Cook the spinach according to the package directions (about 6 minutes) and drain it.

Peel the onion and cut it into ¼-inch pieces. Peel and finely chop the garlic.

Heat the oil in a large frying pan over medium heat. Add the onion and garlic and cook for about 5 minutes, stirring occasionally, until they begin to soften. Add the curry powder, salt, pepper and turmeric and stir until absorbed. Remove from the heat.

Add the rice and spinach and mix thoroughly. The turmeric will turn the rice yellow.

MOM TIP 1

▼

Choose bell peppers that are fat,
rather than long and thin,
because they are easier to stand
on end. If only long, thin peppers
are available, cut them lengthwise
in half, remove the seeds as
directed and lay them on their
sides to stuff them.

MOM TIP 2

▼

Sun-dried tomatoes, which are
tomatoes that have had most of
their moisture removed, are available
in packages in the gourmet
department. They also come
in jars, preserved in olive oil.

Beef / Veal / Lamb / Pork

I ALWAYS GET NERVOUS about cooking meat dishes for company. I worry about the meat being too fatty, too tough or too raw. A lot seems out of my hands, since much is riding on what kind of exercise program the animal was on in the farmyard. I've been to dinners where I had to chew a piece of meat for five minutes and then slyly hide it in my napkin. That's why I don't provide napkins when I entertain.

My mom knows all about the different cuts of meat. But to me, all meats are red and wrapped in plastic. It was a valuable lesson to learn that there's a big difference between a sirloin steak and a round steak. One you serve to the Queen, the other to the dog. Sometimes the ones that look the nicest and juiciest are the toughest. It's important to read the label and buy the cut specified in the recipe. You have to be sure you cook tough cuts long enough. If the directions say to cook at 300 degrees for two hours, don't cook it at 500 degrees for one hour.

Whether you choose Lamb Souvlakia, Beef Bourguignon or Spicy Stir-Fried Orange Beef, it's just about as much work to cook for ten as for two. Of course, it's easier cleaning up for two, but you can't have everything.

▲

Recipes

▼

Beef Bourguignon

SERVES: 4-6

Serve with: Garlic Mashed Potatoes (page 116) ▼ Preparation Time: 20 minutes

Cooking Time: 2-2½ hours ▼ Rating: Not So Easy ▼ Can Prepare the Day Before: Yes

M Y PARENTS USED TO EAT this French version of beef stew in New York in the sixties. I think it made them feel as if they were in Paris in the twenties, with its cafés filled with writers and artists debating the woeful situation of mankind while puffing on cigarettes in foot-long holders. Beef Bourguignon is still sophisticated, but there's no need to bother with the berets and turtlenecks.

1½   pounds beef for stew (see Mom Tip, page 195)

3   garlic cloves

2   tablespoons olive oil

2   cups dry red wine (such as Cabernet Sauvignon, Burgundy, Merlot or Zinfandel; see Mom Tip 1)

1   10-ounce can condensed beef broth

1   tablespoon ketchup

1   bay leaf

½   teaspoon dried thyme

¼   teaspoon black pepper

1   pound medium mushrooms (see Mom Tip 2, page 230)

1   14½-ounce can whole onions or 10-ounce package frozen whole onions (see Mom Tip 2)

1   tablespoon cornstarch or 2 tablespoons all-purpose flour

¼   cup cold water

Cut off and discard any visible fat on the beef. Peel and finely chop the garlic.

Heat the oil in a large flameproof casserole or frying pan over medium-high heat. Add the beef and cook for about 3 minutes, turning the chunks until they are completely browned.

Add the wine, beef broth, ketchup, bay leaf, thyme and pepper and stir. Bring the mixture to a boil, cover and turn down the heat to low.

Cook the beef mixture for 2 hours. Check it once every 30 minutes to make sure the liquid gets no lower than 1 inch deep and stir. Stir in ½ cup water if necessary, but not too much more, or the gravy will be too thin. After 2 hours, the beef should be very tender and easily pierced with a fork. If not, cook it for another 15 to 30 minutes.

Meanwhile, wash the mushrooms, cut away and discard the bottom ¼ inch of the stems and cut the mushrooms in half. If some are much larger than others, cut them into quarters. Set aside.

If you are using canned onions, drain and discard the liquid and set aside. If you are using frozen onions, don't thaw them.

When the beef is tender, add the mushrooms and onions and cook, covered, over medium heat for 5 minutes to warm through.

Mix the cornstarch or flour with the water in a cup and stir well to make sure it is dissolved (see Mom Warning, page 230). Add it to the meat mixture. Continue cooking, stirring frequently, until the liquid comes to a boil and thickens slightly. Remove and discard the bay leaf.

Serve immediately, or let sit, covered, off the heat for up to 30 minutes. Reheat if necessary. Beef Bourguignon reheats very well and tastes even better the second day.

Mom Tip 1

▼

Don't use generic wine labeled "cooking wine," which is the cheapest and possibly the most ill-tasting wine available. Since this dish will pick up the flavor of the wine, use only wine you'd actually drink.

Mom Tip 2

▼

French traditionalists will tell you to buy tiny boiling onions and peel them, but that's a lot of time and trouble. There may be a slight difference in taste, but I prefer the convenience of canned or frozen. Even Kevin's grandmother uses canned onions.

Hungarian Goulash

SERVES: 4

Serve with: Speedy Zucchini (page 144) ▼ Preparation Time: 20 minutes

Cooking Time: 2-2½ hours ▼ Rating: Easy ▼ Can Prepare the Day Before: Yes

GOULASH IS A BEEF STEW with a slightly sweet sauce. I made it for my parents and had to fight my dad for seconds. When my mom served it to her friend Jane, who had just returned from Hungary, Jane said she liked Mom's recipe better than the authentic version she'd just eaten.

1½	pounds beef or veal for stew (see Mom Tip)
2	medium onions
2	tablespoons corn oil or olive oil
¾	cup water
¾	cup ketchup
3	tablespoons Worcestershire sauce
2	tablespoons brown sugar (light or dark)
1	tablespoon cider vinegar
2	teaspoons paprika
½	teaspoon dry mustard

Cut off and discard any fat on the beef or veal. Set aside. Peel the onions and cut them into ½-inch pieces.

Heat the oil in a large flameproof casserole or frying pan over medium heat. Add the onions and cook for about 5 minutes, stirring occasionally, until they have softened.

Push the onions to one side of the pan and add the beef or veal. Turn up the heat to medium-high and brown the meat quickly, turning the chunks to brown on all sides. Add the water, ketchup, Worcestershire sauce, brown sugar, vinegar, paprika and dry mustard and stir. Bring the mixture to a boil, cover and turn down the heat to low.

Cook the meat mixture for 2 hours. Check every 30 minutes to make sure the water hasn't boiled away and stir. Stir in ¼ cup more water if needed, but don't add too much more, or the gravy will be too thin.

When done, the meat should be very tender and easily pierced with a fork. If not, cook it for another 15 to 30 minutes. Serve immediately, or let cool and reheat when needed.

MOM TIP

▼

Stewing beef or veal has been cut into bite-size pieces
and is usually sold in packages near the steaks and roasts.
It's flavorful but tough (and therefore much cheaper than
steak) and requires several hours of cooking to tenderize it.
Veal is generally more expensive than beef, but occasionally,
it's on sale. It's cheaper to cut up your own stewing beef
and the meat will be of better quality. Buy boneless chuck
roast. Don't choose sirloin, porterhouse or other
expensive steaks, which are meant to be
grilled or panfried.

Spicy Stir-Fried Orange Beef

SERVES: 4

Serve with: Spicy Asian Baby Bok Choy (page 150) ▼ Preparation Time: 20-25 minutes

Cooking Time: 6 minutes ▼ Rating: Easy ▼ Can Prepare the Day Before: No

STIR-FRYING IN FRONT OF COMPANY gives a double meaning to the word *entertaining*. A well-organized, calm kitchen can become a whirlwind of food, fire and smoke alarms. When I stir-fried this Chinese beef dish for my grandma, she had a hard time believing my cries of "Everything's under control!" as beef and soy sauce flew into the wok from all directions. When the dust settled and we sat down to eat, she was finally convinced that I didn't need rescuing.

The only advice I have for stir-frying is to set everything you need out on the counter before you turn on the stove, because it's hard to stir with one hand, reach into the cupboard with the other and hold the fridge open with your leg.

1½	pounds sirloin steak (see Mom Tip 1)
1	1-inch piece fresh ginger (see Mom Tip 2) or 1 teaspoon ground
2	garlic cloves
¼	cup soy sauce
2	teaspoons cornstarch or 4 teaspoons all-purpose flour
2	scallions
1	medium zucchini
1	red bell pepper
2	tablespoons peanut oil or corn oil
1	teaspoon dried orange peel (see Mom Tip 3)
½	teaspoon red pepper flakes
¼	cup orange juice + more if needed

Cut off and discard any fat on the beef. Slice the beef into strips ½ inch wide and 2 inches long. Peel and finely chop the ginger and garlic.

Combine the beef, ginger and garlic in a large bowl. Add the soy sauce and cornstarch or flour, mix thoroughly and set aside.

Wash the scallions. Cut off the root tip and top 2 inches of the green parts and discard them. Cut the remaining white and green parts into ½-inch pieces. Wash the zucchini, trim off and discard the ends and cut lengthwise into 4 thin slices. Cut the slices crosswise in half and cut each slice into ¼-inch-wide matchsticks. Wash the red bell pepper, cut it in half and remove and discard the stem and seeds. Slice into ¼-inch-wide strips. Set aside.

Heat 1 tablespoon of the oil in a wok or large frying pan over high heat. Add the dried orange peel and red pepper flakes and cook for about 30 seconds, or until they sizzle. Remove the steak from the bowl with a slotted spoon, leaving behind any marinade in the bowl, and add to the wok. Stir-fry for 3 minutes, stirring continually with a large spoon or metal spatula so that the steak cooks quickly on all sides. When the steak is no longer pink, return it to the bowl containing the marinade.

Heat the remaining 1 tablespoon oil in the wok over high heat and stir-fry the scallions, zucchini and red bell pepper for about 2 minutes, or until they just barely begin to soften. They should stay fairly crisp. Quickly return the steak and remaining marinade to the wok, add the ¼ cup orange juice and bring just to a boil. Add 1 to 2 more tablespoons orange juice if you prefer a thinner sauce. Serve immediately.

MOM TIP 1

▼

Sirloin steak is usually broiled
or grilled on a barbecue, but it's
perfect for stir-fries because
it's boneless and tender.

MOM TIP 2

▼

Fresh ginger is a brown, knobby,
multi-armed root found in the
vegetable department. Break off
as much as you need. In some
produce sections, it is also
available peeled and mashed
in small bottles.

MOM TIP 3

▼

Dried orange peel is available
in the spice aisle. If you can't find it,
substitute 2 teaspoons grated
fresh orange peel.

Sweet-and-Sour Meatballs

SERVES: 4 AS A MAIN COURSE, 8 AS AN APPETIZER

Serve with: Speedy Zucchini (page 144) or egg noodles (see Mom Tip) ▼ Preparation Time: 20 minutes

Cooking Time: 30 minutes ▼ Rating: Easy ▼ Can Prepare the Day Before: Yes

MY MOM SUGGESTED I try this recipe as an appetizer, served with toothpicks. It seemed like an odd way to eat meatballs. I decided to try them as a spaghetti sauce. It was a natural.

MEATBALLS

1 pound lean ground beef (see Mom Tip 1, page 85)

¼ cup dry bread crumbs

¼ cup water

1 large egg

½ teaspoon salt

⅛ teaspoon black pepper

SWEET-AND-SOUR SAUCE

½ cup sugar

1 8-ounce can tomato sauce

¼ cup cider vinegar

¼ cup water + more if necessary

MEATBALLS: Put the ground beef in a large bowl. Add the bread crumbs, water, egg, salt and pepper and mix thoroughly with your hands. Shape the meat mixture into about 60 meatballs, ¾ inch in diameter, and set aside.

SWEET-AND-SOUR SAUCE: Combine the sugar, tomato sauce, vinegar and ¼ cup water in a large frying pan and bring to a boil over medium-high heat.

Add the meatballs, in a single layer if possible, turn down the heat to low and stir gently so that the meatballs are coated with sauce. Cover and cook for 30 minutes, turning after 15 minutes. There should be at least ½ inch of liquid in the pan at this time; if not, add up to ¼ cup more water.

Serve immediately, or let cool and refrigerate until needed. If you do refrigerate the meatballs, remove and discard any hardened fat that has risen to the top of the sauce (it will be bright orange and waxy) before reheating.

MOM TIP

▼

My friend Karen Polansky, who gave me this recipe,
suggests serving the meatballs and sauce with egg noodles.
Egg noodles are a type of dried pasta made with egg
and come in several varieties. "Wide" or "extra-wide"
egg noodles about 2 inches long are easy to eat
and hold gravy or sauce well.

Old-Fashioned Brisket with Barbecue Sauce

SERVES: 4-6

Serve with: Garlic Mashed Potatoes (page 116) ▼ Preparation Time: 5 minutes ▼ Cooking Time: 3 hours

Rating: Very Easy ▼ Can Prepare the Day Before: Yes (preferably; see Mom Tip 1)

BRISKET HAS BEEN A STAPLE in our family for generations. My mom used to eat it at her grandmother's house in the early days of television. The extended family would gather around the set and stare in awe at "I Remember Mama." When I was growing up, my mom continued the tradition, and we'd watch "Family Ties" with amused detachment.

I've recently picked up the brisket habit. My guests don't know about the decades of tradition, but it makes everyone feel at home. And it's an easy way to feed people, which makes me feel at home. My great-grandmother knew what she was doing.

> 1   tablespoon corn oil or vegetable oil
> 1   2-to-3-pound beef brisket (not corned beef brisket; see Mom Tip 2)
> ½   teaspoon salt
> ¼   teaspoon garlic powder
> ¼   teaspoon black pepper
>   Barbecue Sauce, page 203 (optional)

Preheat the oven to 350 degrees.

Heat the oil in a large flameproof casserole or roasting pan over medium-high heat. Put the brisket in, fatty side down, and cook for about 1 minute, or until the fat begins to sizzle. Sprinkle the salt, garlic powder and pepper on top of the brisket. Turn the brisket over and cook for about 30 seconds, or until it browns. Brown the sides in the same way, holding the meat upright with a fork. Turn the brisket fatty side down in the pan and turn off the heat. Add enough water just to cover the brisket. Cover the pot with a tight-fitting ovenproof lid. If you have no lid, cover it tightly with aluminum foil.

Bake for about 3 hours (see Mom Warning). When done, the meat should be very tender and easily pierced with a fork.

Meanwhile, make the Barbecue Sauce, if using.

To slice the brisket, remove it from the liquid and place it flat side down on a cutting board. Cut a thin test slice from one end. If the meat seems very stringy, rotate the brisket a quarter turn and cut another test slice. (You want to cut against the grain rather than with the grain.) Slice the brisket as thin as possible. Serve with the hot Barbecue Sauce or use the cooking liquid as gravy.

MOM TIP 1
▼

Brisket is much easier to slice
thin if it is cold. So, if possible,
cook the brisket the day before
or early in the day and refrigerate it,
covered, until cold. Refrigerating the
gravy will also allow you to remove
and discard any fat that rises to
the top and hardens, although
this is important only if you
are not using barbecue sauce.
If you like brisket and gravy,
reheat the two together.

MOM TIP 2
▼

Brisket is a thin boneless cut of beef.
Whole briskets, which usually weigh
at least 6 pounds, are often sold in
vacuum-sealed plastic bags and may
be labeled "Texas barbecue" or "beef
brisket." Smaller cuts, which are
actually whole briskets cut in half,
are labeled "flat" or center cut and
"point." I prefer the flat, which has
less fat. If only whole briskets are
available, you can: (1) ask the butcher
to cut one in half for you and buy
only half; or (2) buy a whole one,
cut it in half yourself and freeze the
second half for use next month.
If you like corned beef, try cooking
a corned beef brisket, which is red
because it has been "corned," or
soaked in salted water and spices.
It is usually packaged in vacuum-
sealed plastic bags. (Cook it the
same way as fresh brisket. It has a
much saltier flavor.) Serve it
with mustard rather than
Barbecue Sauce.

MOM WARNING
▼

The only thing that can go wrong
in cooking brisket is that all the water
boils away and the brisket burns.
If the lid fits tightly, that is unlikely
to happen. Check on the water level
after about 1½ hours. If there is
less than an inch, add another cup
of water. However, too much
water will result in weak gravy.

Barbecue Sauce

MAKES: ABOUT 4 CUPS

Serve with: Old-Fashioned Brisket (page 200) ▼ Preparation Time: 15 minutes

Cooking Time: 35 minutes ▼ Rating: Easy ▼ Can Prepare the Day Before: Yes

BARBECUE SAUCE makes everything taste better. It takes brisket to another level.

2	medium onions
1	garlic clove
2	tablespoons corn oil or olive oil
2	cups ketchup
¾	cup cider vinegar
½	cup lemon juice
¼	cup water
¼	cup Worcestershire sauce
⅓	cup dark brown sugar
2	tablespoons chili powder
1	tablespoon celery seeds
2	teaspoons ground cumin
2	tablespoons butter or margarine

Peel and finely chop the onions and garlic. Heat the oil in a large pot over medium heat. Add the onions and garlic and cook for about 5 minutes, stirring, until they begin to soften. Add the remaining ingredients except the butter or margarine and stir. Bring to a boil; reduce the heat to medium-low and cook, uncovered, for 30 minutes, stirring occasionally. Add the butter or margarine, stir and remove from the heat. Use immediately, or refrigerate until needed. This sauce will keep for several months.

Veal Scallopini with Mustard Sauce

SERVES: 4

Serve with: Simple Snow Peas (page 140) ▼ **Preparation Time:** 15 minutes

Cooking Time: 10 minutes ▼ **Rating:** Easy ▼ **Can Prepare the Day Before:** No

IN ONE OF MOM'S OLD COOKBOOKS, there's a recipe called "City Chicken," which gives a formula for sculpting veal cubes into the shape of chicken drumsticks. Veal has now become a luxury item, but it has also become an issue for some people. If you're worried about your guests objecting to veal, call them up and casually ask how they feel about foods beginning with V. If they mention an aversion to veal, change the menu.

1¼	pounds veal cutlets (see Mom Tip 1)
3	tablespoons all-purpose flour
¼	teaspoon black pepper
	Dash salt
2	tablespoons butter or margarine
2	tablespoons olive oil
½	cup dry white wine (such as Chardonnay or Chenin Blanc)
¼	cup whipping (not whipped) cream
1	tablespoon Dijon mustard (see Mom Tip 2)

Remove and discard any strips of fat from around the edges of the cutlets. Lay 1 cutlet in the center of a sheet of wax paper, making sure it is as flat as possible, and place another sheet of wax paper on top.

Pound the cutlet with a rolling pin, a hammer or a heavy can until it flattens to a ⅛-inch thickness. Repeat with the remaining cutlets.

Combine the flour, pepper and salt on a large plate and dip each cutlet into the mixture, coating both sides.

Heat the butter or margarine and oil in a large frying pan over medium-high heat. When it is frothy, add as many cutlets as will fit in a single layer and cook for about 2 minutes, or until they begin to brown on the bottom. They will shrink slightly. Turn them over and cook for another 2 minutes. Transfer them to a serving dish and repeat until all the cutlets are cooked. Cover to keep warm.

When all the cutlets are cooked, add the wine to the liquid remaining in the pan and bring to a boil. Add the cream and stir until it comes to a boil. Immediately turn off the heat, add the mustard and stir thoroughly. Pour the sauce over the cutlets and serve.

Mom Tip 1

▼

Veal cutlets, often labeled veal scallopini, are meat with no bones. They are sliced very thin— about ¼ inch thick—and are sold in packages or loose from the butcher's display case. Per pound, veal cutlets are among the most expensive meats sold, but they are easy to cook and impressive to serve.

Mom Tip 2

▼

American-style hot dog mustard is too mild for this dish.

Grilled Leg of Lamb

SERVES: 8-10

Serve with: Spicy Potatoes (page 120)

Preparation Time: 5 minutes (plus heating the grill, if grilling)

Waiting Time: 2 hours (for lamb to reach room temperature before cooking)

Cooking Time: 24-30 minutes ▼ Rating: Very Easy ▼ Can Prepare the Day Before: No

RECENTLY, MY MOM HAD A DINNER PARTY with 18 guests, and at the last minute, she put this recipe together. It was the most successful thing she served that night. I don't have that kind of confidence. If I were cooking for 18 people, I would set the table a week in advance. I tried a smaller version for 4 people, and it was incredibly easy, just as she promised. There were lots of leftovers, but that just meant more for me.

One of the hazards of a big meat dish is having to carve it in front of your guests. You can't just hack it to pieces. With this leg of lamb, you don't have to be Michelangelo with the knife. Just slice it like bread.

1	5-to-6-pound leg of lamb, butterflied (see Mom Tip)
2	garlic cloves
2	tablespoons olive oil
½	teaspoon dried oregano
¼	teaspoon black pepper

Place the lamb flat, fatty side down, on a cookie sheet.

Peel and finely chop the garlic. Put it in a small cup with the oil, oregano and pepper and stir to combine. Spread half the mixture on the lamb. Turn it over and spread the other half on the fatty side. Set aside for about 30 minutes. You can refrigerate it for up to 24 hours, covered. Bring it to room temperature before grilling.

Because this cut has thick and thin parts, you will get different degrees of doneness.

If you plan to grill the lamb outdoors, prepare the grill as described on page 23, with a rack 6 inches from the heat source. Or if you plan to broil the meat in the oven, place the rack about 5 inches from the broiling unit and preheat the broiler.

When the coals are ready or the broiler is hot, place the lamb on the grill rack or place the cookie sheet under the broiler. Grill or broil for 12 to 15 minutes per side, depending on whether you want the lamb rare or well done. When the lamb is cooked, remove it from the grill or oven and set it on a platter or carving board (see Mom Warning). Let it rest for 5 to 10 minutes before slicing.

MOM TIP
▼

"Butterflying" means taking the bones out of a leg of lamb. I always ask someone at the meat counter to do it. Don't be shocked when you open the package and lay the lamb out flat. It will be misshapen, with thick and thin parts, but roughly rectangular. Don't worry. When it's cooked, the thick parts will yield rare slices, while the thin parts will be well done, so you can satisfy everyone at once. The butcher will ask you if you want the bone. You don't need it for this recipe.

MOM WARNING
▼

Don't put the cooked lamb in the same container you used for the raw meat without washing the dish first. You could transfer bacteria to the cooked food.

Lamb Souvlakia

SERVES: 4

Serve with: Lemon Rice (page 122)

Preparation Time: 15 minutes (plus heating the grill, if grilling)

Marinating Time: 30 minutes ▼ Cooking Time: 8-12 minutes

Rating: Very Easy ▼ Can Prepare the Day Before: No

IT'S SAID THAT HISTORY is written by the winners. So is the menu. Case in point: who can name any Trojan delicacies? If the ancient war between Greece and Troy had gone differently, Greek food might not be as well known as it is today. We might be including a recipe for Grilled Trojan Horse instead of Lamb Souvlakia.

Your guests will probably be familiar with some Greek food, like baklava and Greek Salad, but they may not be familiar with Lamb Souvlakia. However, they'll soon see why Greeks going back to Socrates have enjoyed this shish kebab.

2   pounds lean lamb (see Mom Tip)

3   tablespoons olive oil

2   tablespoons lemon juice

1   teaspoon dried oregano

Dash salt

Dash black pepper

8   metal or wooden skewers (see Mom Warning, page 153)

Cut the lamb into 1-inch cubes and remove any fat.

Combine the oil, lemon juice, oregano, salt and pepper in a medium bowl and mix well. Add the lamb and toss so that the cubes are covered with marinade. Cover and refrigerate for 30 minutes.

Place a rack 4 inches from the broiling unit and preheat the broiler. Or prepare the grill as described on page 23, with a rack 6 inches from the heat source.

Thread the lamb onto the skewers and place them on a cookie sheet.

When the broiler is hot or the coals are ready, place the cookie sheet under the broiler. Broil or grill for 4 to 6 minutes per side, depending on whether you like your lamb rare or well done. Serve at once.

MOM TIP

▼

The easiest way to get pieces of lean lamb is to buy
a boneless leg of lamb and cut it into cubes yourself.
A 2½-to-3-pound boneless leg will provide enough
meat for 4 people. Lamb shoulder is too fatty, and
lamb chops cost too much to use this way.

Southern Barbecued Pork

SERVES: 4-6

Serve with: Southwestern Coleslaw (page 100) ▼ Preparation Time: 10 minutes

Cooking Time: 4 hours ▼ Rating: Very Easy ▼ Can Prepare the Day Before: Yes

YOU'VE PROBABLY SEEN THE AD for pork that calls it "the other white meat." To me, that's admitting defeat. How well would the Rolling Stones have done if they'd dubbed themselves "the other pale English band with crooked teeth"? Pork should have taken a more aggressive stance: "Eat pork. Increase your I.Q." This dish is a great way to feed a lot of people and, let's face it, a good alternative to chicken.

PORK

4 garlic cloves

1 3-to-4-pound pork shoulder butt roast (also known as Boston butt)
   or pork shoulder picnic roast (see Mom Tip)

1 cup cider vinegar

12 whole black peppercorns

SAUCE

1 cup cider vinegar

1 teaspoon cayenne pepper

½ teaspoon salt

8-12 sandwich buns (optional)

PORK: Peel the garlic but leave the cloves whole.

Put the pork roast in a large pot. Add the garlic, vinegar, peppercorns and enough water to cover the pork. Bring the liquid to a boil over high heat. Turn down the heat to low, cover and cook for about 2 hours, or until the pork is very tender when pierced with a fork. The meat will have shrunk from the bone.

SAUCE: Meanwhile, combine the vinegar, cayenne pepper and salt in a small bowl. Stir and set aside.

Shortly before the meat has finished cooking, preheat the oven to 350 degrees. Remove the pork from the pot and place it, fat side up, on a rack in a roasting pan. Discard the cooking liquid. Spoon ¼ cup of the sauce over the pork and put it into the oven.

After the pork has baked for 2 hours, remove it from the oven and cut it into thin slices or shreds. It will be falling-apart tender. Serve on a platter with the remaining sauce at room temperature on the side. Eat the pork as is or offer buns so that people can make sandwiches. It's also good with Barbecue Sauce (page 203).

Mom Tip

▼

Because this dish cooks for such a long time,
you can use the cheapest cuts of pork, which come from
the shoulder. Do not use pork loin, or the meat will
be too dry. Leftovers are good in fajitas,
soups and sandwiches.

Sweet-and-Sour Country-Style Pork Ribs

SERVES: 4

Serve with: Caribbean Rice (page 124) ▼ **Preparation Time:** 10-15 minutes

Cooking Time: 1½ hours ▼ **Rating:** Easy ▼ **Can Prepare the Day Before:** No

WHENEVER I MAKE THESE PORK RIBS, I flash back to the good old days of my ancestors, whose idea of a dinner party was to gather around an open fire and cut off chunks of country-style mammoth roasting on a spit. Nowadays, with dining rooms, napkins, plates, silverware and finger bowls, we seem to have lost those primitive gnawing urges. That's why I like to serve these ribs out on the patio. That way, I can get as close to nature as possible.

> 3 **pounds country-style pork ribs (see Mom Tip)**
> **Dash salt**
> **Dash black pepper**
> **Sweet-and-Sour Sauce (page 214)**

Place an oven rack in the middle position and preheat the oven to 450 degrees.

If the ribs are not already separated, cut them apart. Put them on a rack in a roasting pan and sprinkle with the salt and pepper. Cover tightly with aluminum foil and bake for 15 minutes.

While the ribs are baking, make the Sweet-and-Sour Sauce.

Remove the ribs from the oven and turn down the heat to 350 degrees. Discard the foil. Spread about 3 tablespoons sauce on the ribs and bake, uncovered, for 20 to 30 minutes. Turn the ribs over, spread on another 3 tablespoons sauce and bake for 30 more minutes. Turn the ribs over again and spread on a little more sauce, making sure to save some to serve at the table. Bake for 5 minutes more. (This last step can be done on an outdoor grill; see Mom Warning.)

Serve on a platter with the remaining sauce on the side and plenty of napkins.

Mom Tip

▼

Country-style pork ribs, also
called country-style pork strips, are
much thicker and meatier than regular
spareribs. They look more like pork
chops than ribs. Country-style
ribs may be available already cut
into individual ribs or as a rack
(meaning the ribs are lined up
next to each other in one big piece).

Mom Warning

▼

Because of its sugar content,
Sweet-and-Sour Sauce tends to
catch fire on an outdoor grill,
so unless you've prepared the grill
to cook something else—such
as Grilled Vegetable Kebabs
(page 152)—it's not worth the hassle.
However, it is impressive to finish
cooking the ribs over charcoal.
Finish using the grill for other
dishes before taking the ribs out
of the oven. To prevent flare-ups,
do not add any more Sweet-and-Sour
Sauce to the ribs. Grill them for
2 to 3 minutes per side, just
until grill marks show.

Sweet-and-Sour Sauce

MAKES: 1½ CUPS

Serve with: Sweet-and-Sour Country-Style Pork Ribs (page 212) ▼ Preparation Time: 5 minutes

Cooking Time: 10 minutes ▼ Rating: Very Easy ▼ Can Prepare the Day Before: Yes

I'VE ALWAYS BEEN VERY FOND of Sweet-and-Sour Sauce, but I thought you had to order Chinese takeout to get it. It turns out it's easy to make at home and, with the extra kick provided by the mustard, it's even better than what I used to think was already perfect.

- ¾ cup dark brown sugar
- ½ cup prepared mustard
- ¼ cup cider vinegar
- 3 tablespoons molasses (see Mom Tip)
- 1 tablespoon dry mustard

Combine all the ingredients in a small pot. Bring to a boil over high heat, stirring occasionally. Turn down the heat to medium-low and cook, uncovered, for about 5 minutes, continuing to stir, until the sauce is smooth and shiny. Remove from the heat.

MOM TIP

▼

Bottles of molasses are available next to the pancake syrup.

Molasses comes in light and dark versions.

The dark version has a stronger flavor.

Poultry

WHEN PEOPLE GO OUT TO EAT, their first thought usually is, "What nationality?" Italian? Chinese? Canadian? But wherever they end up, the restaurant always serves chicken. In this chapter, we've included recipes from America, India, Indonesia, Mexico, France, Russia and Turkey. Chicken is the real international language, not love. For that reason, chicken is the safest dish to cook for company.

When my parents lived in London in the 1970s, they went to a dinner party held by my father's boss. When they got there, they were surprised to see 1960s-style diner waitresses passing around Colonel Sanders chicken, right from the bucket. Apparently, KFC had just opened in London, and it was very chichi. My parents smiled and complimented the boss on his excellent taste. I don't think I could get away with serving chicken like that. I don't look good in a miniskirt.

▲

Recipes

▼

Barbecued Chicken

SERVES: 4

Serve with: Grilled Vegetable Kebabs (page 152) ▼ Preparation Time: 15 minutes (plus heating the grill)

Marinating Time: At least 2 hours ▼ Cooking Time: 40-50 minutes

Rating: Easy ▼ Can Prepare the Day Before: Partially

THERE'S MORE TO BARBECUING than the rugged man-conquers-fire image. If the food you cook is half-burned and half-raw, your guests won't be in awe of you for very long. Simmering the chicken for a while before grilling it, which you can do before your friends arrive, ensures that you'll save your reputation and they won't have to eat around the middle.

> 4   chicken leg-thigh combinations, 4 breasts, 8 thighs or 12 legs
>   (see Mom Tip 1)
> ¾   cup vinegar (any kind)
> ¼   cup oil (any kind)
> 2   teaspoons salt
> 1   teaspoon poultry or chicken seasoning (see Mom Tip 2)
> ¼   teaspoon black pepper

Put the chicken pieces in a large pot, cover with water, cover and bring to a boil over high heat. Turn down the heat to medium-low and cook breasts for 20 minutes and thighs and/or legs for 30 minutes.

While the chicken is cooking, prepare the marinade. Combine the remaining ingredients in a medium pot and bring to a boil over high heat. Cook for 1 minute. Remove from the heat.

When the chicken has finished cooking, drain it and discard the water. Pour the marinade over the chicken and let it sit for at least 2 hours, or overnight, in the refrigerator.

Prepare the grill as described on page 23, with a rack 6 inches from the heat source.

When the coals are ready, transfer the chicken to the grill rack—save the marinade—and grill for about 10 minutes per side. Spoon some of the marinade onto the chicken pieces when you turn them over. Serve hot. Discard the remaining marinade (see Mom Warning).

Mom Tip 1

▼

When I'm barbecuing, I usually double this recipe because I like to have lots left over. Leftovers can be eaten cold, reheated in the oven the following day or frozen. Leftovers are good with Barbecue Sauce (page 203).

Mom Tip 2

▼

Poultry or chicken seasoning, available in the spice aisle, is a combination of herbs and spices, such as dried garlic, onion, parsley, paprika and red pepper.

Mom Warning

▼

If you want to serve any leftover marinade with the cooked chicken, be sure to boil it for 2 minutes first, because it contains raw chicken juices.

Chicken Satay with Peanut Sauce

SERVES: 4

Serve with: Pacific Rim Rice Pilaf (page 126)

Preparation Time: 30 minutes (plus heating the grill, if grilling) ▼ **Marinating Time:** At least 15 minutes

Cooking Time: 6 minutes ▼ **Rating:** Easy ▼ **Can Prepare the Day Before:** Partially

IN ASIA, peanuts play a large role in fancy cooking. This Indonesian shish kebab is a way of using peanuts that even George Washington Carver didn't dream of.

3	garlic cloves
¼	cup soy sauce
2	tablespoons brown sugar (light or dark)
2	tablespoons light corn syrup (see Mom Tip)
1	tablespoon lemon juice
4	skinless, boneless chicken breast halves (about 1½ pounds)
	Peanut Sauce (page 222)
4	metal or bamboo skewers (see Mom Warning, page 153)

Peel and finely chop the garlic. Put it into a large bowl. Add the soy sauce, brown sugar, corn syrup and lemon juice and stir.

Cut the chicken breasts into strips ½ inch wide and 2 inches long. Add the chicken to the soy-sauce mixture. Stir to coat the strips, cover and refrigerate for at least 15 minutes and as long as 24 hours. While the chicken pieces are marinating, prepare the Peanut Sauce.

You can cook the chicken under the broiler or on an outdoor grill. Place a rack 4 inches from the broiling unit and preheat the broiler. Or prepare the grill as described on page 23, with a rack 6 inches from the heat source.

Thread the chicken pieces onto metal or bamboo skewers and place the skewers on a cookie sheet. When the broiler is hot or the coals are ready, place the cookie sheet under the broiler or transfer the skewers to the grill rack. Broil or grill for about 3 minutes per side. Watch carefully so that they don't over-cook. Transfer the skewers to plates and serve with the Peanut Sauce in a bowl for dipping.

MOM TIP

▼

Corn syrup is a type of liquid sugar.
It is sold in 16-ounce bottles, in light and dark
forms, near the pancake syrup.

Peanut Sauce

MAKES: ABOUT 1 CUP

Serve with: Chicken Satay (page 220) ▼ Preparation Time: 10 minutes

Cooking Time: 5 minutes ▼ Rating: Very Easy ▼ Can Prepare the Day Before: Yes

THIS ISN'T JUST PEANUT BUTTER. It's a highbrow way to flavor everything from Chicken Satay to Grilled Vegetable Kebabs (page 152).

2	garlic cloves
⅔	cup milk + more if necessary
½	cup peanut butter (see Mom Tip 1)
2	tablespoons soy sauce
1	tablespoon lemon juice
1	teaspoon sesame oil (see Mom Tip 1, page 143)
½	teaspoon ground ginger
¼	teaspoon red pepper flakes

Peel and finely chop the garlic. Combine the remaining ingredients in a small pot. Begin heating over medium heat, stirring until the mixture is well combined. Turn down the heat to low and cook for about 2 minutes, stirring occasionally, or until the sauce comes to a boil. It should have the consistency of thick salad dressing. If it seems too thick, add more milk, 1 tablespoon at a time, and stir until it reaches the consistency you want. Remove from the heat and serve. It will keep for 1 week refrigerated.

Mom Tip 1

▼

Either creamy or chunky-style
peanut butter works.

Mom Tip 2

▼

Peanut Sauce can also be used as a
dip for fresh vegetables or as a sauce
for plain cooked broccoli, carrots,
potatoes or leftover cold chicken.
Or try thinning it further with milk
or water and using it as a sauce
for cold cooked noodles.

Mexican Grilled Cornish Hens

SERVES: 4

Serve with: Lemon Rice (page 122) ▼ Preparation Time: 15 minutes (plus heating the grill, if grilling)

Marinating Time: At least 2 hours ▼ Cooking Time: 20-30 minutes

Rating: Easy ▼ Can Prepare the Day Before: Partially

THE REASON TO SERVE Cornish hens is that each guest gets to eat a whole one. Even if you use large hens, everybody gets half a bird, so there's no fighting over white meat and dark meat.

3	garlic cloves
¼	cup olive oil
¼	cup lemon or lime juice
2	tablespoons red wine vinegar
1	teaspoon ground coriander
½	teaspoon ground cumin
½	teaspoon dried thyme
¼	teaspoon red pepper flakes
¼	teaspoon black pepper
	Dash salt
4	small (1½ pounds each) or 2 large (2½ pounds each) Cornish game hens (see Mom Tip 1)

Peel and finely chop the garlic. Combine the garlic, oil, lemon or lime juice, vinegar, coriander, cumin, thyme, red pepper flakes, pepper and salt in a very large bowl or pot. Mix thoroughly. Set aside.

Remove and discard the small bag of giblets from inside each hen and cut the hens in half (see Mom Tip 2). Then cut each half into two pieces: breast-wing and leg-thigh.

Add the pieces to the bowl and spoon the marinade over them. Cover and refrigerate for at least 2 hours, or overnight. Turn the pieces over occasionally so that all the surfaces have a chance to soak up some of the marinade. Transfer the hens to a cookie sheet.

You can cook the hens either on an outdoor grill or under the oven broiler. Prepare the grill as described on page 23, with a rack 6 inches from the heat source. Or place the rack 5 inches from the broiling unit and preheat the broiler.

When the coals are ready or the broiler is hot, transfer the hens to the grill rack or place the cookie sheet under the broiler. Grill or broil for 10 to 15 minutes per side, depending on size. To see whether they're done, cut into a thigh. The juices should be clear, with no pink tinge (see Mom Tip 3).

With small hens, serve 3 to 4 pieces per person. With large hens, serve 2 pieces.

MOM TIP 1
▼

Cornish game hens, also known as Rock Cornish game hens, are actually small chickens. They are usually available frozen near the frozen turkeys. Occasionally, they are available fresh near the chickens. They are often individually wrapped in heavy-duty plastic. If they are frozen, defrost them overnight in the refrigerator.

MOM TIP 2
▼

Because game hens are small, you should have no trouble cutting right through, or alongside, the bones with a sharp knife or kitchen scissors. Don't try to cut, however, until the hens are defrosted.

MOM TIP 3
▼

If the hens are getting too charred but aren't quite done, finish the cooking in the oven, baking them for a few additional minutes at 375 degrees.

Chicken Sultana

SERVES: 4

Serve with: Tabouli Salad (page 102) ▼ Preparation Time: 25 minutes

Cooking Time: 1 hour ▼ Rating: Easy ▼ Can Prepare the Day Before: Yes

CHICKEN SULTANA IS A TURKISH RECIPE. As a Westerner, I know very little about Turkey, but I do know that the Ottoman Empire is not a furniture superstore. The word *sultana* is defined in the dictionary as either the wife, mother or daughter of a sultan or a kind of raisin. Suffice it to say that Chicken Sultana is an unusual chicken dish that doesn't require unusual ingredients.

1	large onion
4	garlic cloves
2	tablespoons olive oil
1	3½-to-4-pound cut-up chicken (see Mom Warning)
1	15-ounce can ready-cut tomatoes
½	cup raisins
2	tablespoons curry powder
½	teaspoon paprika

Peel the onion and cut it into ½-inch pieces. Peel and finely chop the garlic. Set aside.

Heat the oil in a large flameproof casserole or frying pan over medium heat. When it is hot, add as many chicken pieces as will fit in a single layer and cook until they begin to brown, about 5 minutes. Turn them over and cook until the other side browns. If the chicken sticks to the pot, loosen it with a spatula. Transfer the browned pieces to a plate and continue browning the rest of the chicken. When it is browned, transfer it to the plate and set aside.

Remove and discard most of the oil remaining in the pot, leaving about 2 tablespoons. Heat the oil over medium heat, and when it is hot, add the onion and garlic. Cook for about 5 minutes, stirring occasionally, until the onion begins to soften.

Add the tomatoes and their liquid, raisins, curry powder and paprika and stir. Return the chicken to the pot, spoon some of the sauce over it and bring the sauce to a boil over high heat. Turn down the heat to medium-low, cover and cook for 30 minutes. Remove the chicken breasts from the liquid and set aside. Continue cooking the legs and thighs for another 15 minutes. Return the breasts to the pot for 5 minutes to heat up. Serve immediately, or let sit, covered, with the heat off for up to 30 minutes. Reheat if necessary.

MOM WARNING

▼

If you don't like chicken skin, remove it before browning the chicken in the oil.

MOM TIP

▼

If the sauce is too thin, here are two ways to thicken it: (1) transfer as much of the sauce as possible to a small pot. Cook the sauce, uncovered, over medium-high heat for about 5 minutes, or until enough liquid has evaporated to thicken it to your liking. Then return the sauce to the chicken; or (2) dissolve 1 teaspoon cornstarch or 2 teaspoons all-purpose flour in 2 tablespoons cold water. Stir thoroughly, add to the sauce and cook until the sauce boils and thickens.

Chicken with Red Wine

SERVES: 4

Serve with: Garlic Mashed Potatoes (page 116) ▼ Preparation Time: 1 hour (see Mom Tip 1)

Cooking Time: 1½ hours ▼ Rating: Not So Easy ▼ Can Prepare the Day Before: Yes

MY PARENTS DISCOVERED THIS DISH on a trip to Paris 25 years ago. I was a baby at that time, not old enough to consume red wine, even in Paris. But Mom has made it ever since. The alcohol burns off, so I never fell out of my high chair. *Coq au vin*, as this dish is known in France, is a relatively foolproof introduction to French cooking, which has a deservedly high reputation. Your guests will wonder when you had time to take cooking classes.

¼ pound sliced bacon

2 garlic cloves

1 3½-to-4-pound cut-up chicken (see Mom Tip 1, page 236)

3 tablespoons corn oil or olive oil

2 cups dry red wine (such as Cabernet Sauvignon, Burgundy, Merlot or Zinfandel; see Mom Tip 1, page 193)

1 10-ounce can condensed beef broth

1 tablespoon tomato paste or ketchup

1 bay leaf

¼ teaspoon black pepper

½ pound medium mushrooms (see Mom Tip 2)

1 14½-ounce can whole onions or 10-ounce package frozen whole onions (see Mom Tip 2, page 193)

1 tablespoon cornstarch or 2 tablespoons all-purpose flour

¼ cup cold water

Half-fill a small pot with water and begin heating over high heat. Cut the bacon slices crosswise into ¼-inch-wide slivers.

When the water comes to a boil, add the bacon slivers. Turn down the heat to low and cook, uncovered, for 5 minutes. Drain the bacon and set aside.

Peel and finely chop the garlic. Set aside. Trim off and discard any excess fat from the chicken.

Heat 2 tablespoons of the oil in a large flameproof casserole or frying pan over medium heat. When it is hot, add as many chicken pieces as will fit in a single layer and cook for about 5 minutes, or until they begin to brown. Turn them over and cook for another 5 minutes, or until the other side browns. If the chicken sticks to the pot, loosen it with a spatula. Transfer the browned pieces to a plate and continue browning the rest of the chicken.

Return all the chicken to the pot and add the bacon slivers, garlic, wine, beef broth, tomato paste or ketchup, bay leaf and pepper. Bring the mixture to a boil. Turn down the heat to medium-low, cover and cook for 30 minutes.

Remove the chicken breasts from the liquid and set aside. Continue cooking the legs and thighs for another 15 minutes. Remove them from the liquid and set aside. Turn the heat to medium-high and continue cooking the liquid, uncovered, for about 15 minutes, or until the liquid has been reduced by half. (Reducing the liquid makes the flavor stronger.)

Meanwhile, wash the mushrooms, cut away and discard the bottom ¼ inch of the stems and cut the mushrooms in half. Heat the remaining 1 tablespoon oil in a small frying pan over medium-high heat. Add the mushrooms and cook for 3 to 4 minutes, stirring frequently, until they begin to brown. Remove the pan from the heat and set aside.

If you are using canned onions, drain and discard the liquid and set the onions aside. If you are using frozen onions, don't thaw them.

When the chicken liquid has reduced, use a large spoon to skim off and discard the fat that rises to the top. (If you are cooking the chicken the day before you plan to serve it, you can skip this step and instead remove any hardened fat the next day before you reheat the chicken.)

Mix the cornstarch or flour with the water in a cup and stir well to make sure it is dissolved (see Mom Warning). Add the mixture to the chicken liquid and stir until the liquid comes to a boil again and thickens.

Return the chicken to the liquid. Add the mushrooms and their juices and the onions, cover and cook over medium-high heat for about 10 minutes, or until the chicken is hot. Remove and discard the bay leaf.

Serve immediately, or let sit, covered, with the heat off for up to 30 minutes. Reheat if necessary. The chicken reheats very well and tastes even better the second day.

MOM TIP 1

▼

This dish involves a lot of preparation, and I seldom make it unless it's a special occasion. However, it's an excellent choice if you're serving a lot of people, because doubling or tripling the recipe adds only a few more minutes to the preparation time. One time-saving tip is to use 2 casseroles or frying pans to brown the chicken to make the job quicker.

MOM TIP 2

▼

Fresh mushrooms add a nice touch, but you can substitute a 6-ounce can of mushrooms, drained, and eliminate the step of cooking the mushrooms.

MOM WARNING

▼

Never add cornstarch or flour directly to hot liquid, because it will make lumps instead of dissolving. I know, because I've spent hours fishing lumps out of gravy. However, both cornstarch and flour dissolve easily in cold water.

Tandoori Chicken

SERVES: 4

Serve with: Gujerati Beans (page 148)

Preparation Time: 15 minutes (using a food processor) or 20 minutes (by hand)

Marinating Time: At least 6 hours ▼ Cooking Time: 20-30 minutes ▼ Rating: Easy

Can Prepare the Day Before: Partially

AN EAST INDIAN RESTAURANT near our apartment serves great food. But my wife doesn't like to go there because the sedate, family-oriented atmosphere is occasionally shattered by the appearance of a mediocre belly dancer. I don't mind; I'm a supporter of the arts.

To keep the peace, I've learned to make Tandoori Chicken at home. Even though the chicken has to marinate for at least six hours, it's worth the wait. If it's not quite done when your guests arrive, you can stall by practicing your belly dancing for them.

1	medium onion
3	garlic cloves
1	1-inch piece fresh ginger (see Mom Tip 2, page 197)
2	tablespoons lemon juice
1	8-ounce container plain yogurt
2	tablespoons olive oil
2	teaspoons ground coriander
1	teaspoon ground cumin
1	teaspoon salt
¼	teaspoon black pepper
¼	teaspoon ground nutmeg
¼	teaspoon ground cloves

¼ teaspoon ground cinnamon

¼ teaspoon cayenne pepper

4 chicken breasts or 4 leg-thigh combinations

Peel the onion, garlic and ginger. If you have a blender or food processor, grind them with the lemon juice until they are a smooth paste. Or chop them with a knife into ⅛-inch pieces. Transfer the mixture to a large bowl and add the lemon juice.

Add the yogurt, oil, coriander, cumin, salt, pepper, nutmeg, cloves, cinnamon and cayenne pepper to the onion mixture and stir.

Remove and discard the skin from the chicken pieces (see Mom Tip 1). Cut the breasts in half, or cut the legs and thighs apart. Make 2 or 3 deep gashes in each chicken piece and put them into the bowl. Spoon the marinade over the pieces, making sure it gets into the gashes. This will give the chicken more flavor.

Cover and refrigerate the chicken for at least 6 hours, or overnight. Turn the chicken over once or twice during this period.

About 45 minutes before you plan to eat, preheat the oven to 475 degrees. Prepare a cookie sheet by covering it with a sheet of foil (for easy cleanup).

Put the chicken pieces on the foil, keeping as much marinade on them as possible. Discard the rest of the marinade (see Mom Warning).

Bake the chicken breasts, uncovered, for 20 to 25 minutes, or the thighs and legs for 25 to 30 minutes. The chicken is done when it gives off clear, not pink, liquid when pierced with a fork. There is no need to turn the chicken. Remove from the oven and serve.

Mom Tip 1

▼

The skin is removed because
it would keep the spice mixture
from penetrating the chicken.

Mom Tip 2

▼

Tandoori spice mixtures are
available at gourmet food shops
and Indian markets. You can use
1 tablespoon (or more, as directed
on the container) in place of all the
spices. (You'll need to add
the salt, though.)

Mom Warning

▼

The marinade should not be
served on the side or used again,
because it contains raw
chicken juices.

Chicken and Sausage Gumbo

SERVES: 4

Serve with: Corn Bread (page 132) ▼ Preparation Time: 35-45 minutes

Cooking Time: 1 hour ▼ Rating: Not So Easy ▼ Can Prepare the Day Before: Yes

M Y MOM HAS BEEN COOKING this New Orleans-style mix of meat and vegetables since I was little. Now she's passed the recipe on to me. It calls for okra, which is not my favorite vegetable. I have to assume it's an acquired taste that I haven't acquired yet. So I tend to leave the okra out. Nobody complains, leading me to believe that I'm not alone in my preference.

1	large onion
2	large celery stalks
3	garlic cloves
2	tablespoons olive oil + more if necessary
1	3½-to-4-pound cut-up chicken (see Mom Tip 1)
1	15-ounce can ready-cut tomatoes
1	bay leaf
1	teaspoon sugar
1	teaspoon dried oregano
½	teaspoon celery seeds
½	teaspoon red pepper flakes
½	teaspoon salt
½	teaspoon black pepper
¼	teaspoon dried thyme
4	5-to-6-inch-long sausages (see Mom Tip 2)
2	cups frozen sliced okra (see Mom Tip 3)

Peel the onion and cut it into ½-inch pieces. Wash the celery stalks, trim off and discard the ends and cut the stalks into ¼-inch slices. Peel and finely chop the garlic. Set aside.

Heat the oil in a large flameproof casserole or frying pan over medium heat. When the oil is hot, add as many chicken pieces as will fit in a single layer and cook for about 5 minutes, or until they begin to brown. Turn them over and cook for another 5 minutes, or until the other side browns. If the chicken sticks to the pot, loosen it with a spatula. Transfer the browned pieces to a plate and continue browning the rest of the chicken. When it is browned, transfer it to the plate and set aside.

If necessary, add enough oil to the pot to make 2 tablespoons. Heat it over medium heat, and when it is hot, add the onion, celery and garlic. Cook for about 5 minutes, stirring occasionally, until the vegetables begin to soften.

Add the tomatoes and their liquid, bay leaf, sugar, oregano, celery seeds, red pepper flakes, salt, pepper and thyme and stir. Return the chicken to the pot, spoon some of the sauce over it and bring the sauce to a boil. Turn down the heat to medium-low and cook, covered, for 30 minutes.

Meanwhile, prepare the sausages. If they are already cooked, simply cut them into ½-inch-thick slices and set aside. If they are not cooked, put them in a medium pot, cover with water and bring to a boil over high heat. Turn down the heat to medium and cook, uncovered, for 10 minutes. Don't be concerned if foam appears. Drain the sausages, and when they have cooled, cut them into ½-inch-thick slices and set aside.

When the chicken has cooked for 30 minutes, remove the breasts and set aside. Add the frozen okra to the pot, stir, cover and continue cooking for 10 minutes. Add the sausage slices and cooked chicken breasts, stir and continue cooking, covered, for another 5 minutes. Remove and discard the bay leaf. Serve immediately, or let sit, covered, off the heat for up to 30 minutes. Reheat if necessary.

Mom Tip 1

▼

Cut-up chickens are often labeled "best of fryer," which means that the neck and inner workings are not included. The cost per pound is usually considerably more than for a whole chicken, because you're paying for convenience. So if you're trying to save money, buy a whole chicken and cut it up yourself. You will end up with 2 breasts, 2 legs and 2 thighs.

Mom Tip 2

▼

I like hot Italian sausages in gumbo, but any type of sausage, including kielbasa or bratwurst, works well here.

Mom Tip 3

▼

Okra is a popular vegetable in the South and is a standard ingredient in gumbo. Fresh okra is available in some vegetable departments. Choose 1-to-2-inch-long okra, rather than larger ones, which are tougher. Cut off and discard the ends. Cook them whole or cut them into ½-inch-thick slices.

Chicken Kiev

SERVES: 4

Serve with: Gingery Carrots (page 146) ▼ Preparation Time: 30 minutes

Cooking Time: 10 minutes ▼ Rating: Not So Easy ▼ Can Prepare the Day Before: Partially

I'VE HAD CHICKEN KIEV ON AIRPLANES, but the airborne version usually tastes as if it's been sitting too long in the baggage claim. Made well, however, it's impressive enough to serve to the president of your company.

As for the preparation, it may seem counterintuitive to squash a perfectly good chicken breast, fill it with odds and ends and seal it back up. To be sure, it's more complicated than just sticking a whole chicken in the oven. But once your guests taste it, they'll have the same reaction I did: "No wonder the Russians got a man in space first."

1	scallion
2	garlic cloves
2	tablespoons chopped fresh parsley or 2 teaspoons dried
¼	teaspoon dried marjoram
4	skinless, boneless chicken breast halves (about 1½ pounds)
	Dash salt
	Dash black pepper
4	teaspoons butter
¼	cup all-purpose flour
1	large egg
½-1	cup dry bread crumbs
2	tablespoons corn oil or vegetable oil

Wash the scallion. Cut off the root tip and top 2 inches of the green part and discard them. Cut the remaining white and green parts into ¼-inch pieces. Peel and finely chop the garlic. Combine the scallions, garlic, parsley and marjoram in a small bowl. Mix thoroughly and set aside.

Tear off 5 sheets of wax paper about 12 inches long. Lay 4 of them out on a counter. Remove and discard any clumps of fat attached to the chicken breasts and lay a breast in the center of each sheet of wax paper. Make sure each breast is as flat as possible. Place the fifth sheet of wax paper over one of the breasts. Pound the breast with a rolling pin, a hammer or a heavy can until it flattens to a ⅛-inch thickness (see Mom Tip 1). Try to flatten the breast into a circular shape. Place the fifth sheet of wax paper over each breast in turn as you flatten it.

Sprinkle salt and pepper over one side of each flattened breast. Put 1 teaspoon butter in the center of each breast. Spoon one fourth of the scallion mixture onto each piece of butter. Roll up each breast, starting from the narrower end, folding in the ends as you go, so that it looks like a small package. Set aside, seam down, on a large plate. If the breasts won't stay together, fasten each one shut with a toothpick.

Place 3 soup bowls on the counter and add the flour to one, the egg to the second and ½ cup bread crumbs to the third. Beat the egg until frothy.

Coat the rolled-up breasts with the flour. Then dip a flour-coated breast into the egg and roll it in the bread crumbs. Set it on a plate and repeat with the other breasts, adding more bread crumbs to the bowl if necessary. At this stage, you can refrigerate the breasts, covered, for up to 1 day, or you can cook them immediately.

To cook the chicken, heat the oil in a large frying pan over medium heat. Cook the chicken breasts for about 5 minutes on one side, or until they are well browned. Then turn them over and cook for another 5 minutes on the other side. Watch that they don't burn. If they seem to be browning too fast, turn down the heat. Brown the ends briefly by standing the breasts up and keeping them upright with kitchen tongs or a fork or leaning them against the side of the pan for about 30 seconds (see Mom Warning).

Remove the toothpicks, if you used them, and serve immediately (see Mom Tip 2). Warn your guests that when they cut into the chicken, butter may squirt out at them.

Mom Tip 1

▼

Raw chicken breasts are almost
like Play-Doh, although you have
to pound them, rather than press
them, into shape. If a small piece of
chicken (called the tender, or fillet)
separates from the main piece,
overlap the two pieces of chicken
and pound so the fibers meld
together. You want to create a
smooth surface so none of
the filling leaks out.

Mom Tip 2

▼

If necessary, you can keep the cooked
chicken warm in a 200-degree oven,
uncovered, for up to 30 minutes.

Mom Warning

▼

Above all, be sure the chicken
is done in the middle. If you cook
the chicken too long, it will be tough,
but if you don't cook it long enough,
the innermost part will be raw.
Cut into one to make
sure it's done.

Asian Turkey Burgers with Ginger Soy Sauce

SERVES: 4

Serve with: Caesar Salad (page 92) ▼ Preparation Time: 10 minutes
Cooking Time: 5 minutes ▼ Rating: Easy ▼ Can Prepare the Day Before: Partially

I USED TO BE SUSPICIOUS of burgers made of anything but ground beef. Turkey burgers always sounded to me like the meat equivalent of fat-free ice cream—looks the same and is healthier, but just doesn't taste as good. But Asian Turkey Burgers, which include soy sauce and sesame oil, taste better.

They're a perfect food for casual entertaining. They shouldn't be eaten wearing a suit and tie.

    1   **pound ground turkey (see Mom Tip)**
    2   **garlic cloves**
    1   **scallion**
    2   **teaspoons soy sauce**
    2   **teaspoons sesame oil (see Mom Tip 1, page 143)**
  ¼   **teaspoon cayenne pepper**
        Dash black pepper
        Ginger Soy Sauce (page 242)
    4   **sandwich buns**
    1   **tablespoon peanut oil or corn oil**

Put the ground turkey in a large bowl and set aside.

Peel and finely chop the garlic. Wash the scallion. Cut off the root tip and top 2 inches of the green part and discard them. Cut the remaining white and green parts into ⅛-inch pieces.

Add the garlic and scallion pieces to the bowl. Add the soy sauce, sesame oil, cayenne pepper and black pepper and mix well with a fork. Divide the turkey mixture into 4 portions and set aside. You can refrigerate until the next day.

Prepare the Ginger Soy Sauce.

Turn on the oven to 250 degrees and set the sandwich buns on an oven rack to warm.

Heat the oil in a large frying pan over medium-high heat. Scoop up the turkey portions, one at a time, place them in the frying pan and flatten them into thin patties with a fork. If the frying pan isn't big enough to hold all 4 patties at once, cook 2 at a time, keeping the first 2 warm in the oven. Cook for about 2 minutes per side, or until the edges are no longer pink and the burgers are cooked through. Cut into a patty to make sure it is not pink in the middle.

Remove the buns from the oven, slice them in half, if necessary, and place a patty in each. Serve with Ginger Soy Sauce.

MOM TIP

▼

Ground turkey is available fresh in 1-pound packages
in the meat department. It may also be available frozen.
Ground chicken is a fine substitute.

Ginger Soy Sauce

MAKES: ⅓ CUP

Serve with: Asian Turkey Burgers (page 240) ▼ Preparation Time: 5 minutes
Cooking Time: None ▼ Rating: Very Easy ▼ Can Prepare the Day Before: Yes

SEVERAL HUNDRED YEARS AGO, people had to sail around Cape Horn for ginger and soy sauce. Now it's just a trip to Aisle 9 at the grocery store. But that doesn't mean Ginger Soy Sauce is commonplace. It's an easy way to get a little flavor of Asia into your food.

1   ½-inch piece fresh ginger
1   garlic clove
1   scallion
¼   cup soy sauce
2   tablespoons white vinegar
1   tablespoon sesame oil (see Mom Tip 1, page 143)
1   teaspoon sugar

Peel and finely chop the ginger and garlic. Wash the scallion. Cut off the root tip and top 2 inches of the green part and discard them. Cut the remaining white and green parts into ⅛-inch pieces.

Put the garlic and scallion pieces in a small serving bowl. Add the remaining ingredients and mix well.

Seafood

fISH IS A TRICKY DISH to serve to company. It's healthful and tasty, but it's hard to escape the fact that you have to eat around part of the skeleton. You don't want someone to choke on a bone in the middle of the meal. Nothing kills the pleasant atmosphere of a dinner party faster than having to use the Heimlich maneuver.

But there are ways to serve fish without having to post emergency procedures on the wall. Easy Shrimp Creole, of course, has no bones at all, while Crunchy Baked Fish, Greek Island Fish and Grilled Salmon have an occasional large bone that you can take out during preparation. I'm so uptight that I examine the fish with infrared light. But you can skip that step.

▲

Recipes

▼

Easy Shrimp Creole

SERVES: 4

Serve with: Caribbean Rice (page 124; see Mom Tip)

Preparation Time: 15 minutes ▼ Cooking Time: 15-20 minutes ▼ Rating: Very Easy

Can Prepare the Day Before: Partially (add the shrimp just before serving)

THIS IS ONE of my Aunt Betty's favorite recipes. It's a tradition in my family to go to her house to eat this spicy Louisiana-style shrimp dish every Christmas Eve. I don't know where the tradition started, for there's nothing Creole about my Aunt Betty.

Sometimes I cheat and serve this dish at different times of the year. The guests don't seem to mind the Christmas music.

1	small onion
3	garlic cloves
1	red bell pepper
2	tablespoons olive oil
1	bay leaf
1	teaspoon dried oregano
1	teaspoon dried basil
¼	teaspoon black pepper
¼	teaspoon cayenne pepper (less if you don't like spicy food)
	Dash salt
2	15-ounce cans ready-cut tomatoes
1	pound shrimp

Peel the onion and cut it into 1-inch pieces. Peel and finely chop the garlic. Wash the red bell pepper, cut it in half and remove and discard the stem and seeds. Cut the red bell pepper into 1-inch pieces.

Heat the oil in a large pot over medium-high heat. Add the onion, garlic and red bell pepper and cook for about 5 minutes, stirring occasionally, until they begin to soften.

Add the bay leaf, oregano, basil, black pepper, cayenne pepper, salt and tomatoes and their liquid and stir. Continue cooking, uncovered, for another 10 minutes, stirring occasionally. If you're preparing this dish the day before, stop here and refrigerate. Reheat just before serving.

Add the shrimp. If they are already cooked, cook for 1 minute more, just until the shrimp are hot (see Mom Warning). If they have not been cooked, cook for 3 to 5 minutes, or until they are pink and firm, not mushy. Remove and discard the bay leaf. Serve immediately.

MOM TIP
▼

If you want to stretch this dish,
make lots of extra rice and dole out
the portions yourself in the kitchen,
rather than letting guests
serve themselves.

MOM WARNING
▼

Cooked shrimp are ready to eat
when you buy them. Too much
additional cooking will
make them tough.

Greek Island Fish

SERVES: 4

Serve with: Middle Eastern Bulgur Wheat Pilaf (page 130) ▼ Preparation Time: 10 minutes
Cooking Time: 10 minutes ▼ Rating: Very Easy
Can Prepare the Day Before: No

W HEN MY MOM WAS IN HIGH SCHOOL, she went to Greece as an exchange student. She stayed with a family whose last name had 26 letters. Among the meals they cooked for her when they weren't asking for Elvis's home phone number was this basic fish dish. One bite and she knew she wasn't in New Kensington, Pennsylvania, any more.

1½	pounds cod, orange roughy, red snapper or sea bass fillets (see Mom Tip, page 253)
2	large tomatoes
2	garlic cloves
½	cup dry bread crumbs
¼	cup chopped fresh parsley
¼	cup olive oil + more for greasing pan
	Dash salt
	Dash black pepper

Preheat the oven to 350 degrees.

Rub the bottom of a 9-x-13-inch baking pan or cookie sheet with oil. Lay the fish fillets in the pan, making sure they don't touch each other.

Wash the tomatoes and cut them into ¼-inch-thick slices. Peel and finely chop the garlic.

Lay the tomatoes over the fish, covering as much of it as possible. Sprinkle the garlic on top of the tomatoes, then sprinkle the bread crumbs on top of the garlic and the parsley on top of the bread crumbs. Drizzle the oil over the bread crumbs and season with salt and pepper. Bake for about 10 minutes, or until the fish breaks into flakes when you press on it with a fork (see Mom Tip). Serve immediately.

MOM TIP

▼

Cooking time relates to the thickness of the fish.
Each inch of thickness requires 10 minutes of cooking.
Fish is done when it separates into ¼-to-½-inch sections
(flakes) when you prod it with a fork. Undercooked
fish is translucent, and the juices are clear instead
of milky white. If you can see the flakes before
the fork touches the fish, it's overdone.

Grilled Salmon

SERVES: 4

Serve with: Jody's Potato Salad (page 104)

Preparation Time: 5 minutes (plus heating the grill, if grilling)

Cooking Time: 10 minutes ▼ Rating: Very Easy ▼ Can Prepare the Day Before: No

ONE OF THE FIRST TIMES I barbecued for friends, I made grilled salmon, knowing it would be easy. But just after everyone arrived, it started to rain. Smokey the Bear says you can't wheel the barbecue into the house and fire it up in the living room, so I stood out in the rain holding an umbrella over the grill. It was a triumph over nature worthy of a Jack London story. My mom later told me I could have broiled it in the oven, but that's no challenge. Sometimes it's good to show your guests that you're suffering a little.

4	1-inch-thick salmon steaks (see Mom Tips 1 and 2)
¼-½	cup Easy Italian Dressing (page 109) or olive oil
1	lemon

If you are using an outdoor grill, prepare it as described on page 23, with a rack 6 inches from the heat source. If you are broiling the salmon, place an oven rack 4 inches from the broiling unit and preheat the broiler.

Lay the salmon steaks on a cookie sheet and spread a thin coat of dressing or olive oil over the top of each steak. Turn them over and repeat the process.

Wash the lemon and cut it into quarters. Set aside.

When the coals are ready or the broiler is hot, transfer the salmon to the grill rack or place the cookie sheet under the broiler. Grill or broil for 4 to 5 minutes per side (see Mom Tip, page 249); turn gently with a spatula. When done, the fish will be firm to the touch but not falling to pieces. Serve immediately, with a lemon wedge on the side of each plate.

MOM TIP 1

▼

Salmon steaks are slices cut crosswise through
the fish so that each has a piece of backbone in
the middle and skin around the edge. Salmon fillets,
which can also be grilled, are boneless pieces cut from the
sides of the fish, one side of which is covered with skin.
If grilling fillets, place the fillets skin side up on the
grill rack for the first 5 minutes. Then grill skin
side down for another 5 minutes.

MOM TIP 2

▼

Other fish suitable for grilling
include halibut, shark,
swordfish and tuna.

MOM WARNING

▼

Be sure that all the salmon steaks
(or fillets) are of the same thickness
so that they will be done at
the same time.

Crunchy Baked Fish

SERVES: 4

Serve with: Fried Potatoes and Onions (page 114) ▼ Preparation Time: 15 minutes

Cooking Time: 10 minutes ▼ Rating: Very Easy

Can Prepare the Day Before: Yes (but cook just before serving)

AT THE EARLIEST DINNER PARTIES I went to—birthday celebrations hosted by other members of the sandbox social club—fish sticks were the most common entrée. They were a hit—the food most likely not to be thrown across the table. Now that I'm an adult, I can't serve fish sticks. But Crunchy Baked Fish is still a crowd-pleaser. It's fish for people who think they don't like fish.

⅓ cup dry bread crumbs

⅓ cup grated Parmesan cheese

   Dash black pepper

⅓ cup mayonnaise

1½ pounds red snapper, cod, sole or orange roughy fillets (see Mom Tip)

   Tartar Sauce (page 254)

Preheat the oven to 425 degrees. Line a cookie sheet or large baking dish with aluminum foil and set aside.

Combine the bread crumbs, Parmesan cheese and pepper in a soup bowl or on a large plate. Mix well and set aside. Place the mayonnaise in another soup bowl or on a plate. Set aside.

Remove and discard any bones from the fish. Cut each fillet into 2 or 3 relatively equal pieces.

Using a fork, dip 1 fillet into the mayonnaise and coat both sides. Then transfer it to the breadcrumb mixture and coat both sides. Transfer the fillet to the foil-covered cookie sheet or dish and repeat the process until all the fillets are coated.

Bake for 10 minutes, or until the fish breaks into flakes when you press on it with a fork (see Mom Tip, page 249). Serve immediately.

Mom Tip

▼

Fillets are pieces of fish, usually without skin,
that have been cut from the sides of the fish, as opposed
to steaks, which are sliced across the backbone. Fillets of cod,
orange roughy, red snapper and sea bass are fairly thick, about
1 inch or more in the thickest part. They may have
a few bones, but they are big enough to be
removed before cooking.

Tartar Sauce

MAKES: JUST UNDER 1 CUP

Serve with: Crunchy Baked Fish (page 252) ▼ Preparation Time: 5 minutes

Cooking Time: None ▼ Rating: Very Easy

Can Prepare the Day Before: Yes

MY MOM TASTE-TESTED all the tartar sauces in Los Angeles and found that the simplest is best.

¾ cup mayonnaise

2 tablespoons sweet relish

Combine the mayonnaise and relish in a small bowl and mix thoroughly. Serve immediately, or cover and refrigerate until needed.

Brunch

BRUNCH IS THE EASIEST, MOST CASUAL MEAL. It is, in fact, the only one that you can serve with dignity while wearing your pajamas. That doesn't mean you should, unless you have a very healthy self-image. The food itself can be almost anything, although it tends to involve eggs and cheese. But don't let the "br" part of brunch fool you. You can't have people over and serve them a Kellogg's Multipack. Serve them something like Blueberry Waffles or Eggs Benedict instead.

The most filling brunch I ever had was in Edinburgh a few years ago. The meal consisted of bacon, ham, sausage, eggs, black pudding (something involving pig's blood) and a glass of orange juice. In Scotland, if you eat at Denny's, you're a health nut.

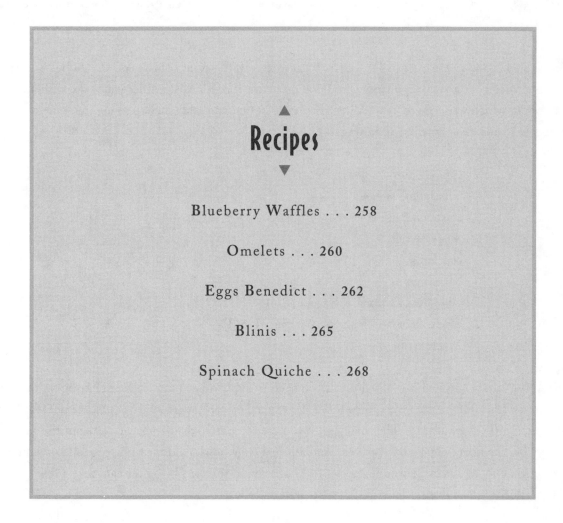

Recipes

Blueberry Waffles

SERVES: 4

Serve with: Apple Crisp (page 272) ▼ Preparation Time: 10 minutes

Cooking Time: 10-15 minutes per batch of waffles ▼ Rating: Easy ▼ Can Prepare the Day Before: No

SOME PEOPLE ARE PERFECTLY HAPPY with frozen waffles, but I think you should be concerned when the toaster is the main appliance you use in preparing a meal. Real waffles you make with a waffle iron (two of which we received as wedding gifts) taste better, and real blueberries are much better than the purple shards that come in frozen waffles.

1¾	cups all-purpose flour
2	tablespoons sugar
2	teaspoons baking powder
¼	teaspoon salt
1½	cups milk
3	large eggs
3	tablespoons corn oil or vegetable oil
1	cup fresh or frozen blueberries (see Mom Tip)
	Maple syrup

Read the directions on your waffle iron. If you need to apply oil or butter before pouring on the batter, do so. If it should be preheated, turn it on. Also check to see how much batter to use per waffle. If you use too little, the waffles will be small, but if you use too much, the batter will ooze out the sides.

Combine the flour, sugar, baking powder and salt in a large bowl. Add the milk, eggs and oil and mix together quickly with a large wooden spoon, whisk or hand mixer. The batter can have a few lumps. Add the blueberries and stir. Make sure they are well distributed.

When the waffle iron is hot, pour on the indicated amount of batter, making sure that the blueberries are well distributed. Close the lid, and if there is a lid lock, snap it shut. Under no circumstances open the waffle iron during the first minute of cooking, because the waffle will separate. Some waffle irons have a light on the front that stays on when the waffle is still cooking. It goes out when the waffle is done. If your waffle iron is like this, check the waffle only after the light goes out. If there is no light, wait until steam has stopped coming out of the sides of the waffle iron.

Check the cooked waffle. If it is softer than you like, let it cook for another 30 to 60 seconds to get crisper. Serve the waffle immediately, with syrup, or keep the cooked waffles warm in a 300-degree oven while you make the rest of them. Lay the cooked waffles directly onto an oven rack, in a single layer, to keep them crisp. Leftovers can be frozen and reheated in a toaster.

MOM TIP

▼

Blueberries are available fresh for only a few months of the year, but frozen berries are available year-round. They can be used straight from the freezer. The heat of the waffle iron will cook them. Wash fresh berries, drain well and remove and discard any stems before adding them to the batter.

MOM WARNING

▼

A waffle iron can be exasperating. Sometimes waffles will come out perfectly, and other times they stick. I finally bought a Salton Belgian Waffle Maker that has a nonstick coating and a light that switches off when the waffle is done. The machine makes only two small waffles at a time, but they always come out perfect.

Omelets

SERVES: 1 (SEE MOM TIP 1)

Serve with: Broccoli, Avocado and Tomato Salad (page 98)

Preparation Time: 1 minute ▼ Cooking Time: 1 minute ▼ Rating: Easy

Can Prepare the Day Before: No

OMELETS ARE THE PERFECT EMERGENCY MEAL. If long-lost friends stop by unexpectedly, it's good to have something you can prepare at a moment's notice, especially if they look sad and hungry. In my younger days, I would have pointed them in the direction of the nearest soup kitchen, but now I can make them omelets, using things I keep around. I always have eggs and cheese, and I usually have something in the vegetable bin to bulk up the omelet. Read the directions several times before starting the omelet, because it will cook so fast you won't have time to refer to them again.

> Filling (optional; see Mom Tip 2)
> 2 large eggs
> Dash salt
> Dash black pepper
> 1 teaspoon olive oil
> 1 teaspoon butter

Choose a frying pan about 7 inches wide at the bottom, preferably with sloping sides so that you can slide the omelet right out onto a plate. It's important that it doesn't stick while it's being cooked, so use a nonstick pan if you have one.

If you're planning to put a filling inside the omelet, prepare the filling and set aside.

Break the eggs into a small bowl and mix lightly with a fork just until the whites and yolks are combined (about 35 strokes). Season with the salt and pepper.

Heat the oil in the frying pan over medium-high heat. Tip the pan so that the oil covers all the inner surfaces. When it starts to sizzle—anywhere from 20 seconds to 2 minutes, depending on the thickness of the pan—add the butter. As soon as the butter melts and begins to froth, a matter of seconds, pour the eggs into the pan.

The eggs will begin to cook immediately. With one hand, jerk the pan back and forth across the burner frequently to keep the omelet from sticking, and with the other, use a fork or metal spatula to lift the edge of the already cooked portion to permit the uncooked eggs to run underneath. Tip the pan to speed this process. All this should happen in about 30 seconds.

While the top of the omelet is still slightly runny (see Mom Warning), sprinkle on any filling. Then fold the omelet over on itself, using a fork or spatula, making a half-moon shape. If it won't fold, slide half of it onto the plate and fold the remaining half over it. Serve immediately.

Mom Tip 1

▼

If you're making omelets for more than one person, cook each individually, one after the other, keeping the frying pan hot and adding another teaspoon of butter each time. You can mix all the eggs together in a large bowl, then measure out and cook ½ cup of the egg mixture at a time.

Mom Tip 2

▼

Omelets are good on their own, but they taste even better with a filling—but no more than ¼ cup, or you won't be able to fold the omelet in half.

Here are some options:

▼ Thinly sliced mushrooms, cooked for 3 minutes in 1 tablespoon butter or margarine.

▼ Grated cheddar, Monterey Jack or Parmesan cheese.

▼ Ham cut into ¼-inch slivers.

▼ Leftover cooked vegetables.

Mom Warning

▼

Overcooking is the biggest problem with omelets. By the time they look done, they're probably overdone. Perfectly cooked omelets may look very moist, but that's the way they're supposed to be.

Eggs Benedict

SERVES: 4

Serve with: Spinach and Strawberry Salad (page 96) ▼ Preparation Time: 10 minutes

Cooking Time: 4 minutes ▼ Rating: Not So Easy ▼ Can Prepare the Day Before: No

MY GRANDMA ALWAYS SERVED Eggs Benedict on Christmas morning, after we opened our stockings but before the big presents. Who could think of food at a time like that? I don't think I actually tasted the eggs until I was 16 or 17, because I'd eat so fast. But once I mellowed out, I realized that the dish is a good alternative to chocolate Santas and candy canes, at least early in the morning. When I serve this myself, I make sure nobody's in a hurry.

Because the eggs, muffins, ham and sauce all have to come together at the end, however, you must do some very quick maneuvering so that all the food is hot but the eggs aren't overcooked.

2 tablespoons white vinegar (see Mom Tip 1)

½ teaspoon salt

1 6-ounce can or jar hollandaise sauce (see Mom Tip 3)

2 English muffins

¼ pound sliced ham (see Mom Tip 2)

4 large eggs

Fill a large deep frying pan almost to the top with water. Add the vinegar and salt and begin heating, covered, over high heat.

Fill a small pot half-full with water and begin heating over medium heat. Open the hollandaise sauce and set the container in the pot, making sure the water comes no more than halfway up its side.

Split the English muffins in half. Divide the ham into 4 equal portions.

Set 4 small bowls or cups on the counter and gently break an egg into each. Set out 4 individual plates or a serving platter. Have a slotted spatula handy.

Now that you've got everything in place, the battle is ready to begin. Start toasting 2 muffin halves— or all 4 if they fit.

Remove the lid from the frying pan. The water should be boiling. If it's not, wait until it is boiling, then turn down the heat to low so it's simmering gently. Carefully pour each egg into a different sector of the frying pan so they don't run together. Put on the lid and turn off the heat. Begin timing the eggs. They should cook for exactly 4 minutes. This procedure is called "poaching" eggs.

As soon as the first batch of muffins is toasted, begin toasting the second batch. Stir the hollandaise sauce and check to see whether it's warm. When it is, turn off the heat but leave the container in the hot water.

When the second batch of muffins is toasted, put the muffins on the plates, smooth side down, and lay the ham on top.

As soon as the timer rings, remove the lid from the eggs. Slip the spatula under 1 egg, lift it gently out of the water, hold it above the frying pan for a few seconds so that excess water drains off and place it on top of the ham. Repeat this process until all 4 eggs are in place.

Spoon 1 teaspoon hollandaise sauce on top of each egg and serve immediately. Offer the extra sauce in a small bowl.

MOM TIP 1

▼

Adding vinegar to the water keeps
the white of the eggs from spreading,
so the poached eggs will be compact
and fit nicely onto the muffins.
Without vinegar, the whites might
spread out 4 to 5 inches.

MOM TIP 3

▼

Leftover cooked ham would be
perfect, but if you don't have any,
buy some sliced Black Forest ham
or other specialty ham at the deli
counter. For vegetarians, substitute
cooked asparagus, spinach or a
handful of shredded cheese.

MOM TIP 2

▼

Hollandaise sauce, which is thick,
rich and lemony, is a perfect topping
for bland poached eggs. I seldom
make my own, though, since
acceptable versions are available in the
gourmet section of the grocery store
or near the Worcestershire sauce.
Once in a while, though, I do make a
quick version in the blender.
Here's the recipe:
In a blender, combine 2 large egg
yolks, 1 tablespoon lemon juice,
¼ teaspoon salt and a dash cayenne
pepper and blend for 10 seconds on
low speed. Melt ⅓ cup butter or
margarine in a small pot over
medium heat and heat until it just
begins to bubble. Turn on the blender
to low speed and slowly pour the
butter through the opening in the lid
onto the egg mixture. Turn off the
blender as soon as the butter has been
added. Use immediately, while warm.

MOM WARNING

▼

Don't cook more than 4 eggs at
once in the frying pan, because the
temperature of the water will cool
down too much to cook the eggs
properly in 4 minutes. If you want to
double this recipe, either use 2 pans
for the eggs or make a second batch
after you've completed the first batch.
A 4-minute poached egg is slightly
runny. If you don't like runny eggs,
leave them in the hot water
for 6 minutes.

Blinis

SERVES: 4

Serve with: Pears in Red Wine (page 274) ▼ Preparation Time: 10 minutes

Waiting Time: 3 hours ▼ Cooking Time: 10 minutes

Rating: Not So Easy ▼ Can Prepare the Day Before: No

STUCK BEHIND THE IRON CURTAIN and deprived of Bisquick, the Russkies came up with their own version of pancakes. They needed a food to put caviar on top of. There was a time in this country when eating Russian food would have been frowned upon ("Save yourself. Just tell us the names of your friends who eat blinis."). But now there are no such worries.

Serving regular pancakes for company might not seem very elegant unless your guests are six years old. But blinis are different. They aren't served with pancake syrup. You don't have to buy caviar; they're plenty good with sour cream. And most people haven't had them before. Experiencing a new kind of food together helps create a sociable atmosphere.

2¼	cups milk
1	¼-ounce package active dry yeast (see Mom Tip 1)
2	cups all-purpose flour
½	teaspoon salt
2	tablespoons butter or margarine
3	large eggs
1	tablespoon sugar
1	tablespoon corn oil or vegetable oil + more as needed (see Mom Tip 2)

TOPPINGS OR ACCOMPANIMENTS:

> Sour cream
> Melted butter
> Plus 1 or more of the following:
> Caviar (see Mom Tip 3)
> Pickled herring
> Smoked salmon
> Jam

Heat 1¼ cups of the milk briefly in a small pot, just to take the chill off; it should be no more than luke-warm (see Mom Warning). Pour the milk into a large bowl and sprinkle the yeast over it. Add the flour and salt and stir thoroughly, but don't worry if there are a few small lumps. The mixture will be sticky.

Cover the bowl with a tea towel, plastic wrap or aluminum foil and set it aside on the counter for 2½ hours, until the batter has more than doubled (an effect caused by the yeast).

When the batter has doubled, melt the butter or margarine in a small pan and set aside.

Separate the eggs (see Mom Tip 1, page 297). Put the egg whites in a large glass or metal bowl (see Mom Warning 1, page 297) and the egg yolks in a medium bowl. Set the egg whites aside.

Add the remaining 1 cup milk, the melted butter or margarine and sugar to the egg yolks and mix thoroughly. Add this mixture to the yeast batter and stir vigorously until everything is well combined. Cover the bowl again and set it aside for 30 minutes.

About 10 minutes before you're ready to eat, beat the egg whites with an electric mixer, an eggbeater or a whisk just until they form stiff peaks. Do not overbeat. Stir the egg whites into the yeast mixture.

Heat the oil in a large frying pan or griddle over medium heat. After 1 minute, flick a drop of water into the pan. If it immediately sizzles, it's time to cook the blinis. If not, wait a few seconds.

Small blinis are easier to cook and turn over, so using about ¼ cup batter per pancake, pour 3 or 4 blinis into the pan. Cook for about 2 minutes, or until the bubbles that appear on the surface of the blinis begin to break. Lift the edge of a blini to make sure the bottom isn't starting to burn. If it is, turn down the heat to medium-low. Flip the blinis over with a metal spatula and cook them for 1 more minute. The second side will not get as uniformly brown.

Serve this batch and immediately start on the second batch. You shouldn't need to add additional oil to the pan, but if the batter starts to stick, add 1 more tablespoon oil. Or if you want to serve everyone at once, you can either: (1) use 2 frying pans to cook the blinis; or (2) keep the cooked blinis hot on a cookie sheet in a 300-degree oven while you cook the rest of the batter.

Serve with sour cream and/or melted butter and one or more of the suggested toppings or accompaniments. Leftover blinis can be reheated in a toaster. Leftover batter can be stored, covered, in the refrigerator for 1 day and then cooked.

MOM TIP 1

▼

Yeast is what makes bread rise. It is most commonly available in dry form, either in 3 foil packets to a strip or in glass jars. You can also buy it fresh, but keep things simple and stick with the strip packages, which are usually found near the flour or in the dairy case. They have a "use-by" date stamped on them. Check to make sure the expiration date hasn't passed.

MOM TIP 2

▼

If you're using nonstick cookware, you don't need to use any oil. However, a little oil will provide extra flavor.

MOM WARNING

▼

Yeast is a living organism, and high temperatures will kill it. Before combining any heated liquid with yeast, test a drop on the back of your hand to make sure it is no hotter than lukewarm.

MOM TIP 3

▼

Caviar's salty taste goes very well with blinis. Real caviar, which are the eggs of a large fish called sturgeon, is hugely expensive and not a luxury you are likely to indulge in often. But there are much cheaper versions available—salmon caviar and red or black lumpfish caviar. They are packaged in 1- or 2-ounce glass jars and are usually available in the gourmet section of the supermarket, at prices varying from $4.00 to $8.00. Use ¼ to ½ teaspoon of caviar per blini.

Spinach Quiche

SERVES: 4 AS A MAIN COURSE, 8 AS A SIDE DISH

Serve with: Fried Cherry Tomatoes (page 141) ▼ Preparation Time: 20 minutes

Cooking Time: 30-35 minutes ▼ Rating: Easy ▼ Can Prepare the Day Before: Yes

MAKING QUICHE is just a matter of mixing and baking. And it's a good use of spinach, a vegetable with an undeservedly low reputation.

Don't worry about serving quiche to company. The nonsense about real men not eating quiche was started in the seventies by some guy who wasn't getting enough oxygen to his brain. I've never had a guest complain about my serving quiche. But maybe none of them was man enough.

1	3-ounce package cream cheese (see Mom Tip 1, page 171)
1	refrigerated pie crust (see Mom Tip)
1	10-ounce package frozen chopped spinach
2	scallions
3	large eggs
½	teaspoon salt
¼	teaspoon black pepper
⅛	teaspoon ground nutmeg

Take the cream cheese out of the refrigerator so that it will begin to soften.

Place an oven rack in the middle position and preheat the oven to 425 degrees.

Place the crust in a 9-inch pie pan and smooth it into place. Cut off and discard any crust that over-hangs the pan. Follow the directions on the package for a "one-crust pie, baked shell." Be careful you don't overbake it; check the crust after it has been in the oven for 6 minutes and every minute or so thereafter until it is lightly browned. Remove from the oven and cool on a rack or the stovetop. Turn down the oven temperature to 375 degrees.

Meanwhile, cook the spinach according to the package directions (about 6 minutes). Drain and set aside.

Wash the scallions. Cut off the root tip and top 2 inches of the green parts and discard them. Cut the remaining white and green parts into ¼-inch pieces.

To make the filling, beat the eggs in a large bowl. Add the cream cheese, spinach, scallions, salt, pepper and nutmeg. Mix thoroughly, making sure there are no large lumps of cream cheese.

Pour the mixture into the pie crust and bake for 25 to 30 minutes, or until the filling is firm and beginning to brown. Remove from the oven and let cool for 5 to 10 minutes before serving.

MOM TIP

▼

These pie crusts come 2 to a box and are located
in the refrigerated section of the grocery store, next to
the tubes of refrigerated biscuits. Pillsbury is a good brand.

DESSERTS

LET'S NOT KID OURSELVES. We all want dessert, and we want it bad. When people come over for dinner, they'll be happy to eat whatever you put in front of them, but there better be dessert at the end. It's like the Fourth of July. Everybody likes the cookout, but what they really want is the fireworks.

▼

One great thing about eating desserts in groups is you feel a lot less guilty. Passing around a Chocolate Cheesecake may be decadent, but you don't feel as sneaky as you do eating a chocolate bar that you've hidden in your desk drawer. Or perhaps I've shared too much.

▲

Recipes

▼

Apple Crisp

SERVES: 4-6

Serve with: Southern Barbecued Pork (page 210) ▼ Preparation Time: 25-30 minutes

Cooking Time: 35-40 minutes ▼ Waiting Time: 30 minutes ▼ Rating: Easy

Can Prepare the Day Before: Yes

THINK OF THIS AS A SLOPPIER, EASIER AND BETTER alternative to apple pie. You don't need decades of experience to make it turn out right. You just throw all the ingredients into a casserole and bake it for 35 minutes.

The only chore is peeling the apples. If you have to peel five or six little ones, it can get a bit tedious. My college friend Paul grew up on an apple farm, and occasionally, his parents would send him a crate of apples, each the size of a human head. They tasted great, but I used to sprain my jaw trying to get my mouth around them. One or two apples that size should do.

    4   large or 6 medium apples
    2   tablespoons lemon juice
    ½   cup (1 stick) butter or margarine
    1   cup dark brown sugar
    ¾   cup all-purpose flour
    1   teaspoon ground cinnamon
        Vanilla ice cream (optional)

Place an oven rack in the middle position and preheat the oven to 375 degrees.

Peel and core the apples (see Mom Tips 1 and 2). Slice the apples into ¼-inch-thick wedges. They will immediately begin to brown, but don't worry about it. Once they're cooked, no one will notice.

Arrange the wedges in layers in a medium (2-quart) baking dish or ovenproof casserole or a large deep-dish pie pan. Sprinkle with the lemon juice.

Put the butter or margarine in a medium bowl and cut into pea-size bits. Add the brown sugar, flour and cinnamon and mix well. Spoon evenly over the apples.

Bake for 35 to 40 minutes, or until the apples can easily be pierced with a fork and the top begins to brown. Let cool for 30 minutes. Apple Crisp is particularly good served warm with vanilla ice cream on the side, but it is also good cold.

MOM TIP 1

▼

The fastest way to peel an apple is with a potato peeler. Start at the stem and peel around the apple in one long strip, trying not to break the skin. If you're lucky, the whole peel will come off in one piece.

MOM TIP 2

▼

The quickest and easiest way to core an apple is to place it stem side down and cut down around the core on all four sides with a knife.

Pears in Red Wine

SERVES: 4

Serve with: Beef Bourguignon (page 192) ▼ Preparation Time: 20 minutes

Cooking Time: 1-1½ hours ▼ Rating: Easy ▼ Can Prepare the Day Before: Yes

PEARS IN RED WINE is one of the few nonchocolate desserts worthy of note. It sounds like a very sophisticated dish, the kind of dessert that the aristocracy might eat following an afternoon of croquet. But don't let that scare you. While it will impress your friends, it's extremely easy to make. And feel free to operate heavy machinery afterwards, as all the alcohol boils off.

- ½ cup sugar
- ½ cup dry red wine (such as Cabernet Sauvignon, Burgundy, Merlot or Zinfandel; see Mom Tip 1, page 193)
- ½ cup water
- 3 whole cloves
- ¼ teaspoon ground cinnamon
- 4 pears (see Mom Tip 1)
  Vanilla ice cream (optional)

Place an oven rack in the middle position and preheat the oven to 400 degrees.

Combine the sugar, wine, water, cloves and cinnamon in a medium pot and bring to a boil over high heat. Turn down the heat to medium-high and boil for 2 minutes. Remove from the heat and set aside.

Peel the pears. Cut off and discard the top ¼ inch of the stem end. Stand each pear on its base and slice it in half through the stem end. With a spoon (see Mom Tip 2), scoop out and discard the circular core, being careful not to cut all the way through the pear. With a knife, cut down each side of the fibrous thread that runs from the stem end to the core. Carefully loosen and discard it.

Place the pear halves, cut side up, in a baking dish. Pour the red wine syrup over them, cover and bake for 1 hour, or until they can easily be pierced with a fork. If you prefer really soft pears, bake them for an extra 30 minutes. Remove from the oven. The pears can be served immediately or left to cool. They can also be served cold.

Put 2 pear halves in each soup bowl and top with a scoop of vanilla ice cream, if using, and 2 to 3 tablespoons of the syrup remaining in the baking dish.

MOM TIP 1

▼

Any type of pear—including Anjou, Bartlett, Bosc and Comice—is suitable for this dessert. The pears should be firm rather than soft and should be unblemished. Very small pears, such as Seckel pears, can be peeled and baked whole. With Seckel pears, plan on 2 per person. The amount of syrup will be enough to cook 8 small pears.

MOM TIP 2

▼

A grapefruit spoon, which has a serrated edge, makes this job very easy.

Gingerbread

MAKES: 16 PIECES

Serve with: Easy Shrimp Creole (page 246)

Preparation Time: 10 minutes (using a food processor or mixer) or 15 minutes (by hand)

Cooking Time: 40-45 minutes ▼ Rating: Easy ▼ Can Prepare the Day Before: Yes

WHEN I WAS YOUNG, my parents would read to me about two twerps, Hansel and Gretel, whose recklessness caused them to be lured into a gingerbread house by a cannibalistic old witch. The message was clear to me: say no to gingerbread.

It turns out I missed the point. Gingerbread is actually an easy and good dessert. And you don't have to shape it into cutesy houses or gingerbread men. Our version is more like brownies.

½ cup (1 stick) butter or margarine, softened to room temperature,
+ more for greasing pan

½ cup sugar

1 large egg

1 cup molasses (see Mom Tip, page 214)

2½ cups all-purpose flour + 1 teaspoon for dusting pan

1½ teaspoons baking powder

1 teaspoon ground ginger

1 teaspoon ground cinnamon

½ teaspoon ground cloves

½ teaspoon salt

Place an oven rack in the middle position and preheat the oven to 350 degrees.

With a food processor: Put the butter or margarine and sugar in the appliance bowl. Process briefly until smooth. Add the egg and molasses (see Mom Tip 1) and pulse for about 10 seconds, or until well blended. Add the remaining ingredients and pulse just until blended. Do not mix the batter too much, or the gingerbread will be tough.

With an electric mixer or by hand: Put the butter or margarine and sugar in a large bowl and mix with the mixer or beat with a wooden spoon until smooth and creamy. Add the egg and molasses and beat just until incorporated. Add the remaining ingredients and mix just until blended. Do not mix the batter too much, or the gingerbread will be tough.

Lightly rub the bottom and sides of a 9-inch square, an 8-inch square or a 10-x-6-inch baking pan with butter or margarine. Add the 1 teaspoon flour (see Mom Tip 2) and swirl it around, coating the buttered surfaces. This coating will keep the gingerbread from sticking to the pan. Pour the batter into the pan.

Bake for 40 to 45 minutes, or until a cake tester or knife inserted into the center comes out clean. Remove from the oven and cool on a rack. Cut into 16 pieces and serve warm or at room temperature.

Mom Tip 1

▼

To keep molasses from sticking
to the measuring cup, first coat the
inside of the cup with corn oil.
All the molasses will
pour right out.

Mom Tip 2

▼

Here's a good way to introduce
a touch of chocolate into your
gingerbread. Instead of using flour
to dust the pan, use cocoa.
Another benefit: cocoa is dark
and won't show on the gingerbread,
as does flour.

Chocolate Shortbread

MAKES: 30-32 COOKIES

Serve with: Mexican Grilled Cornish Hens (page 224)
Preparation Time: 15 minutes (with a food processor)
Cooking Time: 30-35 minutes ▼ **Waiting Time:** 30 minutes
Rating: Very Easy ▼ **Can Prepare the Day Before:** Yes

W HEN JODY AND I visited Scotland, we wanted to bring back exotic gifts for our families. One of the Scots we met suggested that we smuggle in some haggis. Haggis, which is the most famous Scottish food, is the heart, liver and lungs of a sheep stuffed into a sheep's stomach.

But we chose another Scottish delicacy, shortbread. As with most recipes, my mom found a way to make a chocolate version. But I doubt she'll ever attempt a chocolate haggis.

- ¼ cup almonds or hazelnuts
- ½ cup semisweet chocolate chips (or mini chocolate chips if you plan to mix the dough by hand)
- ½ cup sugar
- 1¼ cups all-purpose flour + 1 teaspoon for dusting pan
- ¼ teaspoon salt
- ½ cup (1 stick) butter, softened to room temperature, + more for greasing pan
- 2 tablespoons orange, coffee or chocolate liqueur or vanilla extract (see Mom Tip)

Place an oven rack in the middle position and preheat the oven to 325 degrees.

With a food processor: Grind the almonds or hazelnuts until they are as fine as flour, 1 to 2 minutes, depending on how powerful the machine is, but do not overprocess, or the nuts will be oily. Add the chocolate chips and sugar and process for 1 to 2 minutes, or until the chips are ⅛ inch or smaller.

Add the flour and salt and process for about 10 seconds, or until combined. Add the butter and process for another 10 seconds, or until combined. Add the liqueur or vanilla and process for a final 10 seconds, or just until the dough sticks together.

With an electric mixer or by hand: Place the nuts on a cutting board. Take the largest knife you have, place the tip on the far edge of the board and bring the edge of the blade down through the nuts repeatedly until they are finely chopped (see Mom Tip 3, page 291). Transfer to a medium bowl and stir in the flour and salt. Put the butter and liqueur or vanilla in a large bowl and mix with a mixer or beat with a wooden spoon until smooth and creamy. Add the chocolate chips and mix until incorporated.

Lightly rub the bottom and sides of a 9-inch square, an 8-inch square or a 10-x-6-inch baking pan with butter. Add the 1 teaspoon flour and swirl it around, coating the buttered surfaces. This coating will keep the shortbread from sticking to the pan.

Tip the dough into the pan and press it gently with your fingers or a fork to flatten it and press it to the edges. Bake for 30 to 35 minutes, or until the top is firm and the shortbread begins to pull away from the sides of the pan. Remove from the oven and cool slightly on a rack.

Cut the shortbread into 1-x-2-inch rectangles while still warm, but don't serve until it reaches room temperature. Store any uneaten shortbread in an airtight container.

Mom Tip

▼

Flavored liqueurs, such as Grand Marnier, Curaçao, Cointreau, Kahlúa and crème de cacao, are best known as after-dinner drinks, but they are occasionally used in cooking to provide an intense flavor. Because they are alcoholic, you have to be of age to buy them. They are available in grocery stores in some states and in liquor stores. They come in pint-size or miniature bottles, which are particularly useful for cooking.

foolproof fudge

MAKES: 36 PIECES

Serve with: Asian Turkey Burgers with Ginger Soy Sauce (page 240) ▼ Preparation Time: 5 minutes

Cooking Time: 10 minutes ▼ Waiting Time: 1 hour (or as long as you can wait)

Rating: Very Easy ▼ Can Prepare the Day Before: Yes

FUDGE ISN'T REALLY A NORMAL DESSERT, because the pieces aren't big enough. But it makes an excellent encore to bring out at the very end of the meal, after the regular dessert has been demolished.

Like Indiana Jones, my mom searched the earth for a fudge recipe she could make without messing up. One day, she got an anonymous cooking chain letter that included this recipe. Who knew such things existed? The postmark said New Jersey. Maybe it was from Bruce Springsteen.

3   cups (one and a half 12-ounce packages) semisweet chocolate chips

1   14-ounce can sweetened condensed milk (see Mom Warning)

⅛   teaspoon salt

1   teaspoon vanilla extract

1   cup walnut pieces

Line an 8-inch square, 9-inch square, 9-x-12 or 9-x-13-inch baking dish with aluminum foil (see Mom Tip 1), or rub the bottom of the pan lightly with butter or margarine.

Combine the chocolate chips, condensed milk and salt in a medium pot and begin heating over medium heat. Stir continuously until the chocolate chips have melted, then immediately remove from the heat. Do not let the mixture come to a boil.

Add the vanilla and walnuts and stir thoroughly. Pour the fudge into the prepared pan, smoothing it into the corners with the back of a spoon. Refrigerate until firm, about 1 hour (see Mom Tip 2).

Lift the foil liner and fudge out of the pan. Cut the fudge into 36 pieces and discard the foil. Or if you have not used foil, cut the pieces in the pan and remove them with a spatula. Store the fudge in an airtight container.

MOM TIP 1

▼

The smaller the baking dish, the thicker the fudge will be. If you like thick fudge but have only a large baking dish, pour the fudge into just part of the dish. The mixture is thick enough to stay put.

MOM TIP 2

▼

If you're really desperate, put the fudge in the freezer to cool. It should be ready in about 20 minutes.

MOM WARNING

▼

Sweetened condensed milk, which includes sugar, is different from evaporated milk. It is usually found in the same aisle as the baking supplies, with the rest of the canned milk.

Chocolate Fondue

SERVES: 4-6

Serve with: Grilled Leg of Lamb (page 206) ▼ Preparation Time: 15 minutes

Cooking Time: 10 minutes ▼ Rating: Easy ▼ Can Prepare the Day Before: No

FONDUE IS A VERY SOCIAL WAY TO EAT. When I'm huddled around a fondue pot filled with melted chocolate, I feel like a member of a commune. Another good thing about fondue is that no one knows exactly how much you're eating, so they can't accuse you of taking thirds. Since the goal is finishing the pot, you're just doing your share.

My favorite food to dip in chocolate fondue is strawberries. My mom prefers angel food cake. My sister Bonnie just drinks it with a straw.

CHOOSE 3 OR 4 FROM THE FOLLOWING FOR DIPPING:

Banana slices

Orange sections

Peach slices

Pineapple chunks

Raspberries

Strawberries (cut in half if very large)

Angel food cake

Marshmallows

12 ounces semisweet, bittersweet or milk chocolate (see Mom Tip 1)

½ cup whipping (not whipped) cream

2 tablespoons brandy or rum (optional)

Set up the fondue pot frame and burner attachment on the table and prepare but do not light the burner (see Mom Tip 2). If you have fondue forks (extra-long forks with heatproof handles), set them out. You can also use regular forks, metal skewers or chopsticks.

Wash the fruit. Peel and/or slice as necessary into bite-size pieces. Cut the cake into bite-size pieces. Arrange everything for dipping in small bowls or plates and set on the table.

Break the chocolate into small pieces and put in the fondue pot. Add the cream and brandy or rum and begin heating on the stove over low heat. Stir constantly until the chocolate has melted and the mixture is smooth. Do not let it boil or burn.

Light the fondue burner. Set the fondue pot on the pot frame over the burner. Call the guests.

Mom Tip 1
▼

Chocolate bars or semisweet
baking chocolates work
well for fondue.

Mom Tip 2
▼

A traditional fondue pot is made
of cast iron or stainless steel. It comes
with a frame and burner attachment
that allows you to cook at the table.
Be sure to read the fondue pot
directions carefully and have on hand
the recommended fuel. If you can't
locate a fondue pot, substitute
a small pot that sits on a hot
tray or an electric frying pan
set on low heat.

Chocolate Cake with Buttercream Icing

SERVES: 12-16

Serve with: Old-Fashioned Brisket with Barbecue Sauce (page 200)

Preparation Time: 20 minutes (using a food processor or mixer) or 25 minutes (by hand)

Cooking Time: 35-40 minutes ▼ Rating: Easy ▼ Can Prepare the Day Before: Yes

SINCE MY MOM MAKES THIS CAKE for all the birthdays in the family, I used to wish I had more siblings instead of just one measly sister. It was a good reason to get married, because my wife's July birthday plugs the gap in the summer.

Bakery cakes may look perfect, but the icing usually tastes like grout. I remember at other kids' birthday parties, I would have to choke down the cake to avoid looking like a spoilsport. Our cake may lack the swirls and edible flowers, but the only thing left at the end of the day is the candles.

4	squares (4 ounces) unsweetened chocolate
1	cup dark brown sugar (see Mom Tip 1)
½	cup (1 stick) butter or margarine, softened to room temperature, + more for greasing pan
1	cup sugar
2	large eggs
1	teaspoon vanilla extract
1¼	cups milk
2	cups all-purpose flour + 1 teaspoon for dusting pan
1	teaspoon baking soda (see Mom Tip 2)

½   teaspoon salt
    Buttercream Icing (page 287)

Place an oven rack in the middle position and preheat the oven to 350 degrees.

Melt the chocolate in a small pot over very low heat, stirring constantly. Do not let it boil, or it will become granular and bitter. When it is melted, remove from the heat and add the brown sugar. Stir well to make sure any brown-sugar lumps dissolve. Set aside.

With a food processor: Put the butter or margarine and sugar in the appliance bowl. Process briefly until smooth. Add the eggs and vanilla and process until well blended. Add the chocolate mixture and pulse for about 10 seconds, or until well blended. Add the milk, flour, baking soda and salt and pulse just until blended. Do not mix the batter too much, or the cake will be tough.

With an electric mixer or by hand: Put the butter or margarine and sugar in a large bowl and mix with the mixer or beat with a wooden spoon until smooth and creamy. Add the eggs and vanilla and beat just until incorporated. Add the chocolate mixture and mix well. Add the milk and mix again. Add the flour, baking soda and salt and mix just until blended. Do not mix the batter too much, or the cake will be tough.

Lightly rub the bottom and sides of a 9-x-13-inch baking pan with butter or margarine. Add the 1 teaspoon flour and swirl it around, coating the buttered surfaces. This coating will keep the cake from sticking to the pan (see Mom Warning). Pour the batter into the pan and shake the pan from side to side several times to make sure the batter spreads to all the corners.

Bake for 30 to 35 minutes, or until the cake pulls away from the sides of the pan and a cake tester or knife inserted into the center comes out clean. Remove the pan from the oven and cool for 10 minutes.

Take the cake out of the pan by sliding a knife blade around the edges to loosen the cake. Put a rack on top of the pan, and with a pot holder in each hand, grab the hot pan and rack and turn them over together. Let the cake cool upside down on the rack to room temperature. Turn it right side up and ice when it is completely cool. Or follow the lazy mom's way of icing a cake, which is leaving the cake in the pan and just icing the top.

Mom Tip 1

▼

Sometimes brown sugar gets
hard and you practically have to
chisel it out of the box. Here are
two ways to prevent that:
(1) Once you've opened the box,
transfer the brown sugar to a jar
with a screw top and keep
the jar tightly closed.
(2) After you've opened the box to
remove some sugar, close it again
and place the whole box inside a
self-sealing plastic storage bag.
Store it in the cupboard or
refrigerator. If the sugar is
rock-hard, put it in a pan,
sprinkle it with ½ teaspoon
water and heat it, uncovered, in
the oven at 250 degrees for about
5 minutes. It should soften.

Mom Tip 2

▼

Baking soda is what makes this
cake rise. But nothing happens to it
until it's combined with liquid. Then
it starts bubbling away. So as soon as
you've mixed up the batter, pour
it into the pan and put the
cake in the oven.

Mom Warning

▼

To ensure that you get the cake
out of the pan in one piece, cut a
piece of wax paper to fit the bottom
of the pan. Put it into the bottom of
the pan and grease and flour it.

Buttercream Icing

MAKES: ENOUGH FOR ONE 9-X-13-INCH SHEET CAKE

Serve with: Chocolate Cake (page 284)

Preparation Time: 5 minutes (using a food processor) or 10 minutes (by hand)

Cooking Time: None ▼ Rating: Very Easy

Can Prepare the Day Before: Yes

E VEN THOUGH I LOVE CHOCOLATE, I prefer buttercream icing to chocolate icing. It's perfect with chocolate cake.

½ cup (1 stick) butter, softened to room temperature

1 teaspoon vanilla extract

⅛ teaspoon salt

1 16-ounce box powdered (confectioners') sugar (see Mom Tip 1)

2 tablespoons sour cream or plain yogurt + more if needed (see Mom Tip 2)

With a food processor: Put the butter in the appliance bowl. Process until smooth. Add the vanilla, salt and powdered sugar and process until well blended. The mixture will be very thick. Add the sour cream or yogurt and process until smooth. This may thin the icing enough to make it spreadable, but you'll probably need more to get the right consistency (see Mom Warning).

With an electric mixer or by hand: Put the butter in a large bowl and mix with the mixer or beat with a wooden spoon until smooth and creamy. Add the vanilla, salt and half of the powdered sugar and beat until incorporated. Add the rest of the powdered sugar and beat until incorporated. The mixture will be very thick. Add the sour cream or yogurt and beat until smooth. This may thin the icing enough to make it spreadable, but you may need more to get the right consistency (see Mom Warning).

Put the cake on a serving tray (see Mom Tip 3) and spread on the icing with a wide-bladed knife.

Make sure not to press so hard that cake crumbs are dislodged and mixed in with the icing. Serve cold or at room temperature.

MOM TIP 1

▼

Don't substitute regular sugar, because it won't dissolve.

MOM TIP 2

▼

Instead of sour cream or plain yogurt, you can use whipping (not whipped) cream or milk.

MOM TIP 3

▼

To prevent icing from getting all over the serving tray: *Before* you transfer the cake, cut four 3-inch-wide strips of wax paper, 2 slightly longer than the length and 2 slightly longer than the width of the cake, and lay them on the edges of the empty tray. Then place the cake on top so that each strip is partly under one side. Crumbs and excess icing will land on the wax paper, which can be pulled out and discarded once you've finished.

MOM WARNING

▼

The icing should be thin enough to spread easily but not so thin that it's runny. However, if it's too thick when you try to spread it, pieces of cake will stick to it; add more sour cream or yogurt ½ teaspoon at a time. The ideal consistency is like that of mayonnaise. The icing will dry slightly after it's on the cake. If you inadvertently get a lot of crumbs mixed in with the icing, just pretend they're a decoration and the cake is supposed to be that way.

Chocolate-Raspberry Linzertorte

SERVES: 8-10

Serve with: Chicken Kiev (page 237)

Preparation Time: 15 minutes (with food processor) or 30 minutes (by hand)

Cooking Time: 30 minutes ▼ **Waiting Time:** At least 2 hours ▼ **Rating:** Easy

Can Prepare the Day Before: Yes

THE FIRST TIME I made Linzertorte, an Austrian jam-filled pastry, I wasn't the only one disappointed with the result. When it was time for dessert, our friends' 8-year-old eagerly followed me to the fridge. I should have suspected something was wrong when I had to chisel the granite-hard crust out of the pan. While the adults made conversation and politely ate around the crust, the kid started to bawl. I learned a lesson that evening about the importance of thin crust. Unfortunately, to this kid, I now rank up there with the Grinch Who Stole Christmas. I was the man who stole dessert.

- ¾   cup walnuts
- 6   tablespoons semisweet mini-chocolate chips (see Mom Tip 1)
- ¾   cup all-purpose flour
- 6   tablespoons sugar
- ½   teaspoon salt
- 6   tablespoons (¾ stick) butter or margarine
- 2   teaspoons water
- 1   teaspoon vanilla extract
- 1   cup raspberry jam (see Mom Tip 2)

Place an oven rack in the middle position and preheat the oven to 350 degrees.

With a food processor: Process the walnuts for 15 to 30 seconds, or until they're just a little larger than ⅛ inch. Add the chocolate chips, flour, sugar and salt and process for about 15 seconds, or until thoroughly mixed.

Melt the butter or margarine in a small pot over low heat. Add the melted butter, water and vanilla to the nut mixture and process for about 15 seconds, or just until a dough is formed.

By hand: Put the walnuts on a cutting board. Take the largest knife you have, place the tip on the far edge of the board and bring the edge of the blade down through the nuts repeatedly until they are finely chopped (see Mom Tip 3). Transfer the nuts to a large bowl. Add the chocolate chips, flour, sugar and salt and mix well.

Melt the butter or margarine in a small pot over low heat. Add the melted butter, water and vanilla to the nut mixture and mix with a mixer or beat with a wooden spoon until a dough is formed.

Put the dough in the bottom of a 9-inch pie pan and press it with your hands into an even layer over the bottom and up the sides. Push the dough firmly into the bottom edges of the pan so that it won't be any thicker there (see Mom Warning).

Bake for 15 minutes. Remove from the oven and spoon on the jam, spreading it in an even layer. Bake for another 15 minutes. The jam will be smooth and glistening, and the crust will just be beginning to brown. Remove the pan from the oven and cool on a rack.

Linzertorte tastes good cold or at room temperature. Serve it in thin wedges.

Mom Tip 1

▼

If mini-chocolate chips are
unavailable, use regular chocolate
chips, either whole or chopped
with the walnuts.

Mom Tip 2

▼

Raspberry jam is particularly good
in this dessert, but strawberry jam
is also suitable.

Mom Tip 3

▼

Another way to chop the nuts fine
is to put them in a self-sealing plastic
bag and roll a rolling pin or heavy
can over them several times.

Mom Warning

▼

Avoid making the dough too thick in the bottom
of the pan, or it will be rock-hard. On the other hand,
don't make it so thin that it develops holes.

Chocolate Cheesecake

SERVES: 10-12 (OR MORE)

Serve with: Veal Scallopini with Mustard Sauce (page 204)

Preparation Time: 30 minutes (using a food processor) or 40 minutes (by hand)

Cooking Time: 1 hour ▼ Waiting Time: At least 6 hours ▼ Rating: Not So Easy

Can Prepare the Day Before: Yes

MY WIFE, JODY, AND I love to go to a chain restaurant called the Cheesecake Factory. It has good food, but the cheesecake is what pays the bills for the owner. We drive our ratty old Honda to the valet parking, blush when we hand over the keys and wait forever for a table. But when we reach dessert, it's all worth it.

Chocolate Cheesecake is the most complicated recipe I've made. There are many steps, and my food processor almost had a stroke. But this cheesecake tastes incredibly good. It's the kind of dessert that will leave your guests wowed by your cooking, even if you've burned everything else.

3	8-ounce packages cream cheese (see Mom Tip 1, page 171)
1½	cups chocolate graham cracker crumbs (see Mom Tip 1)
¼	cup (½ stick) butter or margarine + more for greasing pan
12	ounces bittersweet chocolate (see Mom Tip 2)
1	cup sugar
3	large eggs
1	teaspoon vanilla extract
	Dash salt
1	cup light sour cream

Take the cream cheese out of the refrigerator so that it will begin to soften.

Place an oven rack in the middle position and preheat the oven to 375 degrees.

To make the cheesecake crust, grind the graham crackers into fine crumbs in a blender or food processor, or put them in a plastic bag and crush them with a rolling pin or heavy can. Transfer the crumbs to a medium bowl.

Melt the butter or margarine in a small pot over low heat. Add to the crumbs and mix thoroughly.

Lightly rub the bottom and sides of an 8- or 9-inch springform pan (see Mom Tip 3) with butter or margarine. Scrape the crumbs into the springform pan. With your hands, press the mixture firmly over the bottom of the pan and about 1 inch up the sides. Try to make the crust equally thick everywhere. Set aside.

Melt the chocolate in a small pot over very low heat, stirring constantly. Chocolate burns easily, so be careful. Do not let it boil, or it will become granular and bitter. Remove the pot from the heat just before it's completely melted, stir and set aside.

With a food processor: Put the cream cheese in the appliance bowl. Process until smooth. Add the sugar, eggs, vanilla, salt, melted chocolate and sour cream and process until well blended.

With an electric mixer or by hand: Put the cream cheese in a large bowl and mix with the mixer or beat with a wooden spoon until smooth and creamy. Add the sugar, eggs, vanilla and salt and beat until well combined. Add the melted chocolate and sour cream and beat until smooth.

Pour the filling into the crumb crust and shake the pan gently to distribute it evenly. Bake for about 1 hour, or until the top begins to brown. Check it after 50 minutes to make sure the cheesecake hasn't begun to burn. The center may seem a little wobbly, but it will firm up as it cools. Remove the cake from the oven and cool on a rack.

When the cake has reached room temperature, cover the top of the pan with foil or plastic wrap and refrigerate until cold.

To serve, run a knife around the sides of the crust, loosening it from the pan. Remove the sides of the pan. Serve the cake with the base in place. This cheesecake tastes best cold. It keeps well in the refrigerator.

MOM TIP 1

▼

Chocolate graham crackers can
be found on the cookie shelf. Any
plain chocolate cookie can be
substituted, as long it has
no icing or cream filling.

MOM TIP 2

▼

Bittersweet chocolate is slightly
misnamed. It's not bitter at all,
although it's a little richer-tasting
than semisweet and often not quite
as sweet. If you can't find it,
use semisweet.

MOM TIP 3

▼

A springform pan is a deep round
pan, 8 or 9 inches in diameter, with
a bottom that can be separated from
the sides. It's very useful for
cheesecakes and other untraditional
cakes that aren't firm enough
to be tipped out of the pan.
Springform pans are available
at cookware stores.

Lemon Meringue Pie

SERVES: 6-8

Serve with: Grilled Leg of Lamb (page 206) ▼ Preparation Time: 35 minutes

Cooking Time: 15-20 minutes ▼ Rating: Not So Easy ▼ Can Prepare the Day Before: No

L EMON MERINGUE PIE is the opposite of fast food. It requires all your cooking skills, but it's worth it. It's not like running a marathon, where all you get is tired. And homemade is so much better than the store-bought variety.

Unless you're a masochist, you'll probably want to make this in conjunction with an easy meal. Your guests will forgive you for serving them bowls of cereal as a main course once they get to dessert.

3	large eggs
1	refrigerated pie crust (see Mom Tip, page 269)
2	lemons
1	cup + 6 tablespoons sugar
3	tablespoons cornstarch
½	cup cold water
1	cup boiling water
1	tablespoon butter or margarine

Separate the eggs (see Mom Tip 1) and let the whites come to room temperature in a large glass or metal bowl (see Mom Tip 2).

Place an oven rack in the middle position and preheat the oven to 425 degrees.

Place the crust in a 9-inch pie pan and smooth it into place. Cut off and discard any crust that over-hangs the pan. Follow the directions on the package for "a one-crust pie, baked shell." Be careful you don't overbake it; check the crust after it has been in the oven for 6 minutes and every minute or so thereafter until it is lightly browned. Remove from the oven and cool on a rack or the stovetop. Turn down the oven temperature to 400 degrees.

Wash and dry the lemons. Grate the rind against the smallest holes of a grater until the entire yellow surface has been grated off and the white peel shows. Don't grate the white peel; it's bitter. (The lemons will look like golf balls.) Set the lemons aside.

Combine the grated rind, 1 cup of the sugar, the cornstarch and cold water in a medium pot. Stir until the cornstarch is fully dissolved (see Mom Warning, page 230).

Add the egg yolks to the sugar mixture and mix until smooth. Add the boiling water, stirring constantly. Bring the mixture to a boil over medium-high heat, continuing to stir constantly. When the mixture begins to thicken, turn down the heat to medium-low and boil for 2 minutes, continuing to stir. If it's not stirred, the mixture will burn on the bottom.

Remove from the heat, add the butter or margarine and let melt, without stirring. This will take about 5 minutes.

While the butter or margarine melts, cut the lemons in half crosswise and squeeze out the juice. You will have about ½ cup liquid. When the butter or margarine has melted, stir the lemon juice into the filling.

To make the meringue, use an electric mixer, an eggbeater or a whisk to beat the egg whites just until they form stiff peaks. Do not overbeat. Gently beat in the remaining 6 tablespoons sugar, 2 tablespoons at a time, until all the sugar has been absorbed and the peaks have slightly softened. The entire process will take 1 to 2 minutes with an electric mixer or eggbeater, or much longer with a whisk.

Transfer the lemon filling to the baked pie shell. Gently spoon the meringue on top and spread it with the back of a spoon so that it completely covers the filling and touches the edge of the pie crust all around. Swirl the meringue with the back of the spoon to make little peaks.

Bake for 7 to 8 minutes, or until the peaks begin to brown. The meringue is done when it's partly golden brown, partly white. Check after 5 minutes and then every minute thereafter to make sure it does not burn. Cool on a rack. Refrigerate leftovers (see Mom Warning 2).

Mom Tip 1

▼

It's easier to separate eggs when they
are cold. To separate the egg white from the
yolk, have two bowls ready. Crack the egg
firmly against the edge of one bowl; the egg
shell should break in half across the middle.
Separate the two halves, turning them both
upright over the bowl you want to contain the
white. Let the white dribble into the bowl,
keeping the yolk in one upright shell.
By carefully transferring the yolk back and
forth between the shell halves, you can allow
gravity to draw the white into the bowl.
Your goal here is to avoid breaking the yolk.
If any drops of yolk get into the white,
spoon them out, or the beaten whites
won't fluff up properly.

Mom Tip 2

▼

Egg whites can be beaten to a fluffier
state if they are at room temperature.

Mom Warning 1

▼

Avoid plastic or wooden bowls, which may
retain traces of oil. Egg whites need to be
beaten in an absolutely oil-free bowl,
or they won't fluff up.

Mom Warning 2

▼

This pie should be served the day you bake it,
because the meringue may shrink or give off
some liquid after about 12 hours.

Index

About the Authors

KEVIN MILLS, a graduate of Cornell University, lives in Los Angeles, where he is pursuing a career in screenwriting. OK, so he's not alone. But after working on this book, he can write the best dining room scenes in town.

NANCY MILLS, a home economics graduate from Cornell University, frequently employs Kevin as a slave at family dinner parties. Her work has appeared in the *Los Angeles Times, Cosmopolitan, Redbook, Ladies' Home Journal* and *USA Weekend*. She also co-owns a newspaper feature syndicate.

Kevin and Nancy's previous collaboration was *Help! My Apartment Has a Kitchen Cookbook* (Houghton Mifflin).